Programme
for the
Formation of Priests
in
Irish Seminaries

IRISH BISHOPS' CONFERENCE

VERITAS

Published 2006 by
Veritas Publications
7/8 Lower Abbey Street
Dublin 1
Ireland
Email publications@veritas.ie
Website www.veritas.ie

ISBN 1 85390 928 9

Designed by Colette Dower
Printed in the Republic of Ireland by Betaprint, Dublin

*Veritas books are printed on paper made from the wood pulp of managed forests. For
every tree felled, at least one tree is planted, thereby renewing natural resources.*

Contents

Abbreviations

AA   Vatican II, Decree on the Apostolate of Laity, *Apostolicam actuositatem* (18 November 1965)

AAS   *Acta Apostolicae Sedis: commentarium officiale*

AG   Vatican II, Decree on the Church's Missionary Activity, *Ad gentes* (7 December 1965)

CCC   *Catechism of the Catholic Church* (1994)

CIC   *Code of Canon Law* (1983)

CL   Post-Synodal Apostolic Exhortation, *Christifideles laici* (30 December 1988)

DMLP Congregation for the Clergy, *Directory on the Ministry and Life of Priests, Tota ecclesia* (1994)

DMR   Congregation of Bishops, *Directives for the Mutual Relations between Bishops and Religious in the Church* (1978)

DPSE Congregation for Catholic Education, *Directives Concerning the Preparation of Seminary Educators* (1994)

DV   Vatican II, Dogmatic Constitution on Divine Revelation *Dei verbum* (18 November 1965)

EB   *Enchiridion Biblicum, Documenta Ecclesiastica Sacram Scripturam Spectantia*, Naples (1961)

EN   Pope Paul VI, Apostolic Exhortation *Evangelii nuntiandi* (8 December 1975)

EVT   Congregation for the Doctrine of the Faith, *Instruction on the Ecclesial Vocation of the Theologian, Donum veritatis* (1990)

FC   Pope John Paul II, Apostolic Exhortation *Familiaris consortio* (22 November 1987)

FR   Pope John Paul II, Encyclical Letter *Fides etrRatio* (14 September 1998)

GS   Vatican II, *Pastoral Constitution on the Church in the Modern World, Gaudium et spes*

ICEL   International Commission on English in the Liturgy

ILFS   Congregation for Catholic Education, *Instruction on Liturgical Formation in Seminaries* (1979)

IVT   Congregations for Catholic Education, for the Oriental Churches, for Institutes of Consecrated Life and Societies of Apostolic Life. *New Vocations for a New Europe, In Verbo tuo,* Final document of the Congress on Vocations to the Priesthood and to the Consecrated Life in Euope (May 1997)

LG   Vatican II, Dogmatic Constitution on the Church, *Lumen gentium*

MP   The Second General Assembly of the Synod of Bishops, Document on *Ministerial Priesthood, Ultimis temporibus* (30 November 1971)

NA   Vatican II, Declaration on the Relationship of the Church to Non-Christian Religions, *Nostra aetate* (1965)

OD   The Roman Pontifical (ICEL, 1978) *Ordination of a Deacon*

OP   The Roman Pontifical (ICEL, 1978) *Ordination of a Priest*

OT   Vatican II, Decree on the Training of Priests *Optatam totius* (28 October 1965)

PCV   *Development of Pastoral Care for Vocations in the local Churches, experiences of the past and programmes for the future* – The Conclusive Document, Rome (1981)

PDV   Pope John Paul II, Post-Synodal Apostolic Exhortation *Pastores dabo vobis* (25 March 1992)

PO   Vatican II, Decree on the Ministry and Life of Priests *Presbyterorum ordinis* (7 December 1965)

PTCM   Congregation for the Clergy, *The Priest and the Third Millennium Teacher of the Word, Minister of the Sacraments and Leader of the Community* (1999)

RF   Congregation for Catholic Education, *Ratio fundamentalis institutionis sacerdotalis* (19 March 1985)

RM   Pope John Paul II, Encyclical Letter *Redemptoris missio* (7 December 1990)

RP   Pope John Paul II, Post-Synodal Apostolic Exhortation *Reconciliatio et paenitentia* (2 December 1984)

SC   Vatican II, Constitution on the Sacred Liturgy *Sacrosanctum concilium* (4 December 1963)

TCL   Congregation for Catholic Education, *On the Teaching of Canon Law to Those Preparing to be Priests* (1975)

TFFP   Congregation for Catholic Education, *The Theological Formation of Future Priests* (1976)

TFR   The Second Extraordinary General Assembly of the Synod of Bishops, *The Final Report* (1985)

VC   Pope John Paul II, Apostolic Exhortation *Vita consacrata* (25 March 1996)

VQA   Apostolic Letter of John Paul II on the 25th Anniversary of the Promulgation of Sacrosanctum Concilium, *Vicesimus quintus annus*, (1989)

Chapter I

The Identity and Mission of the Priest

A Divine Call

1.   'Priests exist and act in order to proclaim the Gospel to the world and to build up the Church in the name and person of Christ the Head and Shepherd.'[1] This is a responsibility and honour which no one takes 'upon himself, but he is called by God'.[2] It is Christ himself who chooses and calls his priests, in the same way as he called his first disciples. 'You did not choose me, but I chose you.'[3] God calls his priests in love, exactly as he called Abraham to found a new people, Moses to free Israel and above all Mary to be the mother of the Saviour. The Church recognises this divine initiative of love in its official welcome of the candidate for the priesthood when she prays 'may God who has begun this good work in you bring it to completion'.[4]

2.   Christ calls people to ministry through the ministry of those he has already called. His call reaches them through the dialogue of love between God and his people which is the life of the Church. 'All things have been delivered to me by my Father; and no one knows the Son except the Father, and no one knows the Father except the Son and anyone to whom the Son chooses to reveal him.'[5] The dialogue of God's loving gift of himself is the birthplace of the vocation to be a Christian and of the vocation to be a priest. The Church is the home where this dialogue takes place and therefore the whole Church is priestly: 'the entire Church participates in the priestly anointing of Christ in the Holy Spirit'.[6] Within the Church and by the power of the Holy Spirit, the bishop lays hands on those who are called by God to the ministerial priesthood and prays the prayer of consecration over them.

---

[1] PDV 15
[2] Heb 5:4
[3] Jn 15:16
[4] OD 16; OP 16
[5] Mt 11:27
[6] DMLP 1

3.   This is why *Pastores dabo vobis* says that 'the priest's identity ... like every Christian identity, has its source in the Blessed Trinity'.[7] The Church's own identity is to be a mirror of the love, harmony, wisdom and power of the Holy Trinity. The identity of her priests is equally trinitarian and ecclesiological. A seminary, where students are prepared for the priesthood, must form them in a trinitarian and an ecclesiological way. Thus, they will be able to make the churches they serve reflections of the life of the Trinity. 'The communion of Christians with Jesus has the communion of God as Trinity, namely, the unity of the Son to the Father in the gift of the Holy Spirit, as its model and source, and is itself the means to achieve this communion: united to the Son in the Spirit's bond of love, Christians are united to the Father.'[8]

Sharing in Christ's Priesthood

4.   The priesthood of sacred ministers shares in the unique priesthood of Christ, made priest and mediator through the offering of his own sacrifice once and for all on the cross.[9] 'On the cross, Jesus showed himself to the greatest possible extent to be the Good Shepherd who laid down his life for his sheep.' Through his death and resurrection, Christ exercised a supreme and unique priesthood which surpassed 'all the ritual priesthood and holocausts of the Old Testament'.[10] As perfect mediator and ideal priest, he bore the sins of the whole world and entered the heavenly sanctuary.[11] By rising from the dead and being made Lord,[12] he reconciled us to God; and he laid the foundation of the people of the new covenant, which is the Church.'[13]

5.   Christ alone is Priest, with a priesthood that all his followers share. The fundamental reality of the priesthood is Christian existence; the identity of the ordained priest has its roots in Christian identity. With Christ the Priest as their head the whole Church offers worship, sacrifice and glory to God. The people's role in the Eucharistic celebration shows their priestly function clearly. Here they participate with the leader of the celebration – a member of the order of the priesthood – in joining themselves to the sacrifice of Christ. This action embraces and draws up into itself all the sacrifices and offerings of their lives.

---

[7] PDV 12; cf. PDV 11–18
[8] CL 18
[9] Cf. Heb 7:27
[10] MP I, 1; cf. PDV 13

[11] Cf. Heb 8:1–6; 9:11–14, 24–28; 10:11–14, 19–25
[12] Cf. Phil 2:9–11
[13] MP I, 1

6.   Nevertheless, as the Second Vatican Council states, while the ministerial priesthood and the priesthood of all believers come from the one priesthood of Jesus Christ, 'they differ essentially and not only in degree'.[14] Thus, 'the priesthood of priests while presupposing the sacraments of initiation is nevertheless conferred by its own particular sacrament. Through that sacrament priests, by the anointing of the Holy Spirit, are signed with a special character and so are configured to Christ the priest in such a way that they are able to act in the person of Christ the Head.'[15] Priests share 'ontologically' in the priesthood of Christ. This means that priests are configured to Christ, not just in virtue of what they do, but in virtue of who they are. They are 'deeply and fully immersed in the mystery of Christ'.[16] At the heart of ordained priesthood is its relation to Christ as Head and Shepherd of the Church. Priests are priests because Christ has said to them, 'as the Father has sent me, even so I send you'.[17]

7.   The common priesthood and ministerial priesthood are both means of sharing in the unique priesthood of Christ. The ordained priesthood is specifically instituted by Christ to serve the common priesthood of the baptised. 'The ministry of the priest is entirely on behalf of the Church; it aims at promoting the exercise of the common priesthood of the entire people of God.'[18]

8.   The identity and mission of the priest are rooted in Christology: reference to Christ is the absolutely necessary key for understanding the priesthood.[19] Christ is the visible, tangible and totally accessible expression of God's plan to save every person. It is within this perspective of the saving will of God who in Christ wishes to save every person that the priest finds his deepest identity. In this sense, he is called to be a sacrament, a sign and instrument of the limitless openness of the heart of God eternally turned outwards to all humankind and to all creation. The perfect expression of the universal outreach of Christ is his death on the cross.[20]

9.   When the Church affirms that the priest is *alter Christus*[21] it does not mean merely Christ's representative, rather that the figure of Christ has been stamped on his very soul.[22] The sacramental character of Holy Orders empowers the minister to put on the mind of Christ and act *in persona Christi*. Thus, through the

---

[14] LG 10
[15] PO 2
[16] PDV 18
[17] Jn 20:21
[18] PDV 16

[19] PDV 12
[20] Cf. PDV 21
[21] Pope John Paul II, *Letter to Priests on Holy Thursday* (18 March 1991), 2
[22] CCC 1563

priest, Jesus renews his paschal sacrifice, forgives sins and communicates his grace. Hence, the priestly attitude of mind is especially that of Christ in his death on the cross: the attitude of complete gift of himself to the Father and complete gift of himself to the service of all men and women. This is what the formation of candidates for the priesthood chiefly seeks to impart. Thus the priest becomes an instrument of life's renewal and authentic human progress. The priest continues to proclaim Christ's Good News to the world so that Christ may continue to be present and to minister to his pilgrim people.

10.   'As a visible continuation and sacramental sign of Christ'[23] the Head of the Church and intimately united as co-workers with the bishops, priests are commissioned in a unique way to continue Christ's mission as prophet, priest, and king.[24] Their primary duty is to proclaim the Gospel to the whole world by word and deed. In this way the priest is a minister of the word, *nomine Christi et nomine Ecclesiae*.[25] This mission extends to all people, even those for whom the Gospel has ceased to be a message of hope or a challenge to right action.[26] The preaching of the Gospel finds its source and culmination in the Eucharist.[27]

11.   As members of the one presbyterate gathered around the bishop, priests serve to unite the local church in one great act of worship of the Father. They preside at the celebration of the Eucharist which is the everlasting renewal of Christ's sacrifice on the cross, and at the other sacraments (apart from Confirmation of which the bishop is the Ordinary Minister and Holy Orders which is reserved to the bishop alone). The Eucharist is 'the beginning, means and end of the priestly ministry'.[28] Most clearly, priestly identity shines forth in the highest way. The whole priestly ministry draws its strength from this one sacrifice.[29]

12.   Priests exercise the office of shepherd, in virtue of the 'specific ontological bond which unites the priesthood to Christ the high priest and Good Shepherd'.[30] Called to gather into one the people of God, priests act with a spiritual authority that enables them to build up and serve the Church.[31] In this way, they are servants of Christ present in the Church.[32]

---

[23] PDV 16
[24] PO 14
[25] PTCM 2
[26] PO 4
[27] PO 5; LG 11; TFR 1

[28] DMLP 48
[29] CCC 1566
[30] PDV 11
[31] PO 6
[32] PDV 16

13.   As Pope John Paul II has expressed it, 'by sharing in the anointing and in the mission of Christ the priest is able to continue Christ's prayer, his word, his sacrifice and his saving action in the Church. All this enables him to serve the Church as mystery because he brings about the sacramental signs in virtue of which Christ is present and active in the Church. He is also the servant of the Church as communion because he is united to the bishop and to his fellow priests for the purpose of building up the unity of the Church in the harmony of the various vocations and gifts and services with which the Holy Spirit endows her. Finally he is a servant of the Church as mission because he enables the community to proclaim and be a witness to the Gospel.'[33]

Ordained into Communion

14.   All Christian life is steeped in a sense of communion. Already, in the Old Testament the saving love of God is always revealed to his people as a community, from the vocation of Abraham[34] to the final renewal of the Covenant in the prophets.[35] Jesus too called a group of disciples to live a common life with him. The twelve are more than the mere sum of twelve individuals, they are a true living community gathered round the Master.[36] Accordingly, the Second Vatican Council described the Church as 'the people of God, the body of Christ, the bride of Christ, the temple of the Holy Spirit, the family of God'.[37] These images, in their different ways, 'bring to light the reality of the Church as a communion with its inseparable dimensions: the communion of each Christian with Christ and the communion of all Christians with one another'.[38]

15.   This means that the priest's relation to Christ is the basis of his relation to the Church. The priest's specific relation to the Church is one of service.[39] 'The priest exists not only *in* the Church but also *for* the Church.'[40]

16.   The priest must always remember that he is pastor in the Church, for the Church and of the Church. When Christ chooses someone to be a priest, he calls him to be a minister of the community which was formed by him, that is, of his Church, built on the rock of Peter[41] to whom he entrusted the care of his sheep.[42]

---

[33] Ibid.
[34] Cf. Gen 12:2
[35] Cf. Ez 8:8
[36] Cf. Mk 3:14; Jn 6:70–71; Jn 20:24; 1 Cor 15:5
[37] LG 6
[38] CL 19; cf. TFR, II, C, 1: 'The ecclesiology of

communion is the central and fundamental idea of the Council's documents.' Cf. also PDV 12
[39] PDV 16
[40] Ibid.
[41] Cf. Mt 16:18
[42] Cf. Jn 21:15–17

Outside of the Church the priest's mission loses its meaning. 'How is it going to be possible to love Christ without loving the Church, since the most beautiful testimony given concerning Christ is that of St Paul, "He loved the Church and gave himself up for her."'[43] The priest loves the Church following the example of Christ's great love for her. His Christian and priestly vocation was born in the Church and is nourished by her. He is therefore aware that he has been chosen by Christ as a priest of the Church and for the Church and that she has confirmed this choice and has consecrated him in the name of God.

17.   So, 'an ecclesiology of communion becomes decisive for understanding the identity of the priest, his essential dignity, and his vocation and mission among the People of God and in the world'.[44] Moreover, 'membership in and dedication to a particular Church does not limit the activity and life of the presbyterate to that Church: a restriction of this sort is not possible given the very nature both of the particular Church and of the priestly ministry ... for every priestly ministry shares in the universality of the mission entrusted by Christ to his apostles'.[45] While it is the college of bishops in union with the Pope that is primarily responsible for the mission of the Church both *ad intra* and *ad extra*, every priest by ordination is sacramentally inserted into communion with the bishops and with other priests, for service of the whole people of God. As the Second Vatican Council says: 'Christ sent the Apostles as he himself had been sent by the Father, and then through the Apostles made successors, the bishops, sharers in his consecration and mission. The function of the bishops' ministry was handed over in a subordinate degree to presbyters so that they might be appointed in the order of the presbyterate and be co-workers of the episcopal order for the proper fulfilment of the Apostolic mission that had been entrusted to it by Christ.'[46]

18.   Priests, as ministers of the sacraments, share the diocesan bishop's ministry of sanctifying God's people. The Second Vatican Council speaks of priests as ministers who do not have 'the supreme degree of priesthood' and who, in exercising their ministry, depend on bishops. Still, they are associated with them 'by reason of their priestly dignity'.[47] Priests, like bishops, bear 'the image of Christ, the supreme and eternal priest'.[48] Therefore they participate in Christ's pastoral authority: this is the characteristic note of their ministry, based on the

---

[43] Eph 5:25; EN 16
[44] PDV 12
[45] PDV 32

[46] PO 2; CCC 1562
[47] LG 28; cf. CCC 1564
[48] LG 28

sacrament of Orders conferred on them. 'The ordained ministry has a radical "communitarian form" and can only be carried out as a "collective work".'[49]

Evangelisation and Mission

19.   The task of evangelisation 'demands priests who are deeply and fully immersed in the mystery of Christ and capable of embodying a new style of pastoral life, marked by a profound communion with the Pope, the bishops and other priests, and a fruitful cooperation with the lay faithful, always respecting and fostering the different roles, charisms and ministries present within the ecclesial community'.[50] All the members do not have the same function within Christ's body, the Church.[51] Speaking of the nature and mission of the priesthood, Pope John Paul II states that 'the priest ... is configured in his being to Jesus Christ, Head and Shepherd, and shares in the mission of preaching the good news to the poor in the name and person of Christ himself'.[52]

20.   The anointing of the Holy Spirit in the sacrament of Holy Orders is conferred through the hands of the bishop, thereby joining the priest 'to the other members of this presbyterate on the basis of the sacrament of Holy Orders and by particular bonds of apostolic charity, ministry and fraternity'.[53] At the Last Supper Jesus prayed that the community of his followers be a reflection and participation in trinitarian community.[54] The price of the communion Jesus established in his Church is his sacrifice on the cross. Priests too can only experience communion by paying the price of fidelity and patience.

21.   The priest is incardinated into a particular Church or presbyteral community.[55] His incardination constitutes an authentic juridical bond.[56] Thus, the priest is 'inserted into the *Ordo presbyterorum* constituting that unity which can be defined as a true family in which the ties do not come from flesh nor from blood but from the grace of Holy Orders'.[57] Pope John Paul II has emphasised that 'the priest's relationship with his bishop in the one presbyterate, his sharing in the bishop's ecclesial concern and his devotion to the evangelical care of the

---

[49] PDV 17
[50] PDV 18
[51] Cf. Rom 12:4; PO 2
[52] PDV 18
[53] PDV 17
[54] Jn 17:11

[55] CIC 265
[56] Cf. Pope John Paul II, Address in the Cathedral of Quito to Bishops, Priests, Religious and Seminarians (29 January 1985): *Insegnamenti*, VIII/1 (1985), 247–253
[57] DMLP 25; cf. PDV 74

People of God in the specific historical and contextual conditions of a particular church' is of great importance in the priest's spiritual life.[58]

22.   Priests by virtue of their vocation are called to 'consecrate their free will to the service of God and their fellow Christians, accepting and carrying out in a spirit of faith the commands and suggestions of the Pope, their bishop and other superiors'.[59] This is not the blind obedience of a servant but the collaborative assent of one marked with 'the glorious liberty of the children of God'.[60] It is not a blind, passive or unwilling subjection but an attitude of active, dynamic and joyful filial love. The priest must therefore be a man of the Church profoundly and cordially at one with the universal Church and the diocesan bishop. One of his tasks is to transmit this spirit of collaboration to God's people so that together they may create a genuinely united church.

23.   While a priest is incardinated into a particular Church or presbyteral community, his pastoral ministry must be universal in principle and intention: it must be intrinsically missionary.[61] In virtue of the sacrament of Orders, the *Catechism of the Catholic Church* states, 'priests share in the universal dimension of the mission entrusted by Christ to the Apostles'.[62] A vision of the local Church that is too narrow must be overcome so as to foster instead the community spirit that is open to the horizons of the universal Church. 'The spiritual gift which priests have received in ordination does not prepare them merely for a limited and circumscribed mission, but for the fullest, in fact the universal mission of salvation to the end of the earth. The reason is that every priestly ministry shares in the fullness of the mission entrusted by Christ to the Apostles'. By the very nature of their ministry they should therefore be penetrated and animated by a profound missionary spirit and 'with that truly Catholic spirit which habitually looks beyond the boundaries of diocese, country or rite, to meet the needs of the whole Church, being prepared in spirit to preach the gospel everywhere.'[63] Seminarians must be helped during their formation to understand the relationship between the particular and the universal Church, the missionary vocation of every priest and the special missionary vocations within the Church.[64]

---

[58] PDV 31
[59] PO 15
[60] Rom 8:21
[61] RM 67; PDV 32

[62] CCC 1565
[63] PDV 18; cf. PO 10 and OT 20
[64] PO 10; PDV 16

Spirituality of the Priest

Baptism and Ordination

24.   While all Christians are called to holiness by their Baptism, the sacrament of Orders establishes a specific call to priestly holiness. It consecrates priests to God in a new way and makes them the living instruments of Christ the eternal high priest. 'The relation of the priest to Jesus Christ and in him to his Church, is found in the very being of the priest, by virtue of his sacramental consecration/anointing, and in his activity, that is in his mission or ministry.'[65] Thus, the spiritual life of priests does not refer to an aspect of their life but to the whole of it – ministerial and personal – grasped and lived from its deepest source, the priests' relationship to Christ and the Church. Priests continue the proclamation of the kingdom by preaching, sanctifying and leading God's people, fulfilling the roles to which they were especially commissioned at ordination. They do the same by the witness of their own lives as celibate men, prayerful, obedient to God's will and simple in lifestyle. For priests, the call to holiness therefore represents a responsibility closely linked to their identity, ministry and spirituality. 'For it is through the sacred actions that they perform every day, as through their whole ministry which they exercise in union with their bishop and their fellow priests, that they are set on the right course to perfection of life.'[66]

Counsels of Perfection

25.   In order to fulfil their vocation to holiness in and through their ministry, diocesan priests look to the counsels of perfection as important guidelines in their own spiritual lives. 'The teaching and example of Christ provide the foundation for the evangelical counsels of chaste self-dedication to God, of poverty and of obedience.'[67] Rooted in the life and ministry of Jesus, these counsels have been joined over the centuries to many forms of Christian spirituality. In regard to diocesan priesthood, they represent 'a particularly significant expression of the radicalism of the Gospel'.[68] They help to formulate the meaning of a priestly way of life in which celibacy, obedience, simplicity of

---

[65] PDV 16
[66] PO 12; CIC 276

[67] LG 43
[68] PDV 27

life and prayer play a role. None of these elements can be properly understood in isolation from the others. Rather, they influence one another and are interwoven as parts of an integral priestly life, helping diocesan and all other priests fulfil their vocation to lead holy lives in and through their ministry.

Celibacy

26.   The celibate commitment remains one of the most fundamental expressions of Jesus' call to radical discipleship for the sake of the kingdom.[69] From a Christian point of view, celibacy is not the denial or repression of sexuality. However, a willingness to live without wife and family – as Jesus did – is a positive and strong witness to the kingdom. Even this highest and most cherished natural good, a family, is transformed in light of God's kingdom. The reality of that kingdom, unseen and intangible, yet present in the life of the resurrected Jesus, becomes the touchstone on which a new life is built. Thus for priests, the absence of natural family and genital sexual activity is replaced by other ties of affection, respect and love, which take on heightened meaning in light of the presence of God's kingdom. This heightened relationship that the celibate priest has with his people prefigures how we will experience the fullness of God's kingdom in heaven. At its deepest point, celibacy can be called 'a sign and motive of pastoral charity, and a special source of spiritual fruitfulness in the world',[70] because the celibate commitment means a consecration to God by which a priest 'adheres more easily to Christ with an undivided heart'.[71] This, in turn, renders him more focused in his ministry.

Poverty or Simplicity of Lifestyle

27.   For diocesan priests, the evangelical counsel to poverty takes on a distinctive meaning: the call to simplicity of life.[72] The priests of the New Testament are, it is true, by their vocation to ordination, set apart in some way in the midst of the People of God, but this is not in order that they should be separated from the people, but that they should be completely consecrated to serving people. They could not be servants of Christ unless they were witnesses and dispensers of a life other than that of this world. So their very ministry invites them not to conform themselves to this world.[73] On the other hand, they would

---

[69] LG 42
[70] LG 42; cf. PO 16; OD 14
[71] OD 2

[72] PDV 30
[73] Cf. Rom 12:2

be powerless to serve the people if they remained aloof from their life and circumstances.[74] Although they do not take vows of poverty, diocesan priests are challenged to view creation as God's gift thereby acquiring 'a right attitude to the world and to earthly goods'.[75] Such an attitude is not disparaging of the world but sees it in light of freedom and service. Priests have responsibility towards personal and parochial finances and property. This enables them to understand correctly 'that the Church's mission is carried out in the midst of the world and that created goods are absolutely necessary for one's personal progress'.[76] They can also better appreciate that when the desire for acquisition and possession is controlled, the human capacity for appreciation and enjoyment of the world can be enhanced. Having fewer possessions and being less burdened by the demands they impose, one can put on more easily the mind and heart of Christ, which gives true freedom and perspective. They should live among people in this world and, as good shepherds, they should know their sheep and should also seek out those who have strayed and those who do not belong to this fold, so that they too may hear the voice of Christ.[77] In the pursuit of this aim priests will be helped by cultivating those virtues which are rightly held in high esteem in human relations. Such qualities are goodness of heart, sincerity, strength and constancy of mind, careful attention to justice, courtesy and other qualities which the apostle Paul recommends when he says: 'Whatever is true, whatever is honourable, whatever is just, whatever is pure, whatever is lovely, whatever is gracious, if there is any excellence, if there is any worthy of praise, think about these things'.[78]

28.   A priest's lifestyle should manifest a healthy balance of physical exercise, study and leisure. It should also manifest a discerning approach to reading, cinema, television, information technology and other forms of educational and leisure pursuits.[79]

Obedience and Authority

29.   A unique characteristic of diocesan priesthood is the special relationship of priests to the bishop of the diocese.[80] Priests promise obedience and respect to their bishop and his successors.[81] The bishop's authority and the priest's

---

[74] PO 3; cf. Jn 17:16; Pope Paul VI, Encyclical Letter *Ecclesiam suam*, AAS 56, (1964) 627, 638

[75] PO 17; cf. DMLP 67

[76] PO 17

[77] Cf. Jn 10:14–16; PO 3

[78] Phil 4:8; PO 3

[79] Cf. RF 68

[80] PDV 28

[81] OP 16

obedience are central to the unity and vital to the mission of the local church. Consequently, a sound understanding of both is crucial for a healthy spirituality among diocesan priests. Fundamentally obedience is an attitude of heart which facilitates detachment from one's own agenda and allows the priest to exercise his ministry as a co-worker with the bishop.

30.   The Gospels provide a new model of authority and obedience: the master is to be the servant of all. Power in human terms is transformed into service.[82] Authority exercised in such terms elicits a special response of obedience. The latter means a willingness to hear others and to respond faithfully in imitation of Christ who came first to do the will of the Father who sent him[83] and who in the garden of Gethsemane, said to his Father, 'Not as I will, but as thou wilt'.[84]

Practical Guidelines

31.   To enable priests to 'put on the mind of Christ' and to foster union with Christ in all circumstances of life, they have at their disposal the means both common and particular, new and old, which the Holy Spirit has never ceased to raise up among the people of God and which the Church recommends to all in living out the call to holiness.[85]

32.   Jesus 'in the days of his flesh … offered up prayers and supplications with loud cries and tears'.[86] So the priest, to live as Jesus lived, should pray as Jesus prayed.[87]

33.   Like all the baptised, priests are to draw nourishment pre-eminently from the double table of holy Scripture and the Eucharist. 'Since they are ministers of the Word, they read and hear every day the Word of God which they must teach to others. If they strive at the same time to make it part of their own lives, they will become daily more perfect disciples of the Lord.'[88] Through meditation on the Word of God, priests fulfil the exhortation of the bishop on the day of ordination: 'Share with all the word of God you have received with joy. Meditate on the law of God, believe what you read, teach what you believe, and put into practice what you teach.'[89] The priest 'needs to approach the word with a docile and prayerful heart, so that it may deeply penetrate his thoughts and feelings and bring about

---

[82] Cf. Jn 13:12–17
[83] Cf. Jn 4:34; 5:30; 6:38
[84] Mt 26:39; cf. Mk 14:36; Lk 22:42
[85] Cf. PO 18

[86] Heb 5:7
[87] Cf. DMLP 39
[88] PO 13; cf. DV 25
[89] OP 14

a new outlook in him – "the mind of Christ" – such that his words and his choices and attitudes may become ever more a reflection, a proclamation and a witness to the Gospel'.[90]

34.   'If the service of the Word is the foundational element of the priestly ministry, the heart and vital centre of it is constituted, without doubt, in the Eucharist, which is, above all, the real presence in time of the unique and eternal sacrifice of Christ.'[91] 'For the priest, the truly central place, both in his ministry and spiritual life, belongs to the Eucharist, since in it is contained 'the whole spiritual good of the Church, namely Christ himself our Pasch and the living bread which gives life to men through his flesh – that flesh which is given life through the Holy Spirit. Thus people are invited and led to offer themselves, their works and all creation to Christ.'[92] In the Eucharist priests are drawn to imitate the mystery they celebrate and model their lives on the mystery of the Lord's cross.[93]

35.   'From the various sacraments, and in particular from the specific grace proper to each of them, the priest's spiritual life receives certain features. It is built up and moulded by the different characteristics and demands of each of the sacraments as he celebrates them and experiences them.'[94]

36.   As Jesus praised his Father in prayer, so do his priests as they continue his mission in the world. Following the example of Jesus who prayed for the community of believers, priests pray with and for the Church they serve. This they do when they 'celebrate faithfully the Liturgy of the Hours for the Church and for the whole world'.[95] For the Liturgy of the Hours is the song of praise which shapes a life of prayer around the mysteries of the Lord celebrated in the liturgical year.

37.   Along with liturgical prayer, the priest should find time regularly for personal prayer and reflection. 'Following the example of Christ, the priest must know how to maintain the vivacity and abundance of the moments of silence and prayer in which he cultivates and deepens his own essential relationship with the living figure of Jesus Christ.'[96] To his prayer, the priest should be careful to add fasting and almsgiving so that his living may be in harmony with the Sermon on the Mount and the tradition of the Church.

---

[90] PDV 26
[91] DMLP 48
[92] PDV 26; PO 5
[93] Cf. OP 26

[94] PDV 26
[95] OD 15
[96] DMLP 40

38.   Like any good member of the faithful, the priest needs to confess his own sins and weaknesses. He is the first to realise that the practice of the Sacrament of Reconciliation reinforces his faith and charity towards God and his brothers and sisters.[97] Indeed, 'the priest's spiritual and pastoral life, like that of his brothers and sisters ... depends, for its quality and fervour, on the frequent and conscientious personal practice of the Sacrament of Penance ... the whole of his priestly existence suffers an inexorable decline if by negligence or for some other reason he fails to receive the Sacrament of Penance at regular intervals and in a spirit of genuine faith and devotion. If a priest were no longer to go to confession or properly confess his sins, his *priestly being* and his *priestly action* would feel its effects very soon, and this would also be noticed by the community of which he was the pastor.'[98]

39.   Along with the Sacrament of Reconciliation, the practice of spiritual direction is recommended to priests 'in order to contribute to the improvement of their spirituality'. 'Through these practices, they will enlighten the conscience, from the first steps in the ministry, and realise the importance of not walking alone along the paths of spiritual life and pastoral duties.'[99]

40.   Despite the urgent demands of the active ministry, priests are encouraged to place a high value on time for retreat and recollection, and for regular spiritual reading. Under the light of a faith that has been nourished by regular silence and recollection and by spiritual reading, 'priests can diligently search for the signs of God's will and the inspirations of his grace in the varied events of life. In this way they will become daily more docile in the demands of the mission they have undertaken in the Holy Spirit'.[100]

41.   In Mary, Mother of Jesus Christ and Mother of priests, priests find a wonderful example and model of total dedication, under the guidance of the Holy Spirit, to the mystery of the redemption of all humanity. 'And so priests are called to have an ever firmer and more tender devotion to the Virgin Mary and to show it by imitating her virtues and praying to her often.'[101] Through this devotion they will be led to a growing love for her Son and they will find a support for their celibate commitment and their humble service of others for the sake of the kingdom.

---

[97] Cf. DMLP 53
[98] PDV 26; RP 31
[99] DMLP 54

[100] PO 18
[101] PDV 82

Chapter II

THE VOCATIONAL JOURNEY

Starting Point: The Christian Community

42.   Vocation to the priesthood is part of the wider field of Christian vocation. 'Each of us is called by our baptism and confirmation to play a unique part in the work of Christ and his Church.'[102] Through Baptism the Church is established by Christ as a fellowship of life, charity and truth: it becomes thus an instrument for the redemption of all and is sent forth as 'the light of the world and the salt of the earth'.[103] Every vocation comes from the Holy Spirit who, 'according to his own richness and the needs of the ministries, distributes his different gifts'[104] for the building up of the Body of Christ with its 'flourishing variety of members and functions'.[105] The ministerial priesthood is one of these gifts and it is of vital significance for the Church. By this vocation a Christian is chosen by God[106] to a special participation in the priesthood of Christ in order 'to nourish the Church by the word and grace of God'.[107]

43.   'Every member of the Church, excluding no one, has the grace and the responsibility of caring for vocations.'[108] So all Christians, and especially priests, must ensure that the faithful are led individually in the Holy Spirit to a development of their own vocation[109] so that they 'may reach their Christian maturity'.[110]

44.   As God is the source of every consolation and author of every vocation, so 'every vocation is born from in-vocation'[111] and 'the hinge of the whole programme of vocations promotion is *the prayer demanded by the Saviour*'.[112] We

---

[102] *Come Follow Me*, Irish Bishops' Pastoral (1989), p. 2
[103] Cf. Mt 5: 13–16
[104] Cf. 1 Cor 12:1–11
[105] LG 7
[106] OT 2

[107] LG 11; PDV 23, 26, 48; DMLP 48
[108] IVT 25; cf. OT 2
[109] PO 6
[110] Ibid.; PCV 18
[111] IVT 27
[112] Cf. Mt 9: 28; IVT 25

must pray unceasingly to the Lord of the harvest, that he will send workers to his Church in order to meet the needs of the new evangelisation.'[113]

45.　'The first responsibility for the pastoral work of promoting priestly vocations lies with the bishop, who is called to be the first to exercise this responsibility even though he can and must call upon many others to co-operate with him.'[114] The bishop cannot act alone. Bishops, priests and faithful, who are called to holiness and have all equally received the faith that leads them to justice in God[115] are united with each other, in the selection of candidates to the priesthood.

46.　Parish communities are crucially important in promoting vocations. 'The European Congress on Vocations has proposed one objective among others: to bring pastoral work for vocations into the life of the Christian parish communities, where people live and where young people in particular are involved to a greater or lesser extent in an experience of faith.'[116]

47.　The pastoral care of vocations at parish level consists essentially in letting young people begin to participate in a concrete and active manner in the life and mission of the parish. The vocational search takes place especially in the parochial community in which young people have a responsible part.

48.　In this way young people discover how to establish a living community, how to listen to the Word of God, how to perform catechesis, how to pray and how to serve both the Church and humanity. While they need guidance and assistance, they must consider themselves true protagonists, according to their personal charisms and within each one's capabilities: 'They themselves ought to become the prime and direct apostles of youth, exercising the apostolate among themselves and through themselves, and reckoning with the social environment in which they live.'[117] Their contribution extends beyond the world of young people. Others too can benefit from it: for example, the poor, the elderly, the marginalised, the abandoned.

49.　Working thus in the community, the young people discover the reality around them and the ministries and services which the community needs. Then,

---

[113] VC 64
[114] PDV 41
[115] Cf. 2 Pet 1:1; LG 32

[116] IVT 73; cf. Pope John Paul II, Encyclical Letter *Novo millennio ineunte* (2001), 46
[117] AA 12

if it is the Lord's plan, these experiences may lead to a more permanent commitment. Experiencing faith and Church in a way that is profound and total 'leads every believer to the discovery and assumption of his own responsibility in the Church',[118] and some to earnestly discern whether they are called to total dedication to Christ and to service of others in the ministerial priesthood – 'to make a radical commitment to a life of love, of prayer and of justice in following Jesus Christ'.[119]

Youth Organisations

50.　Today, Catholic youth organisations, liturgical groups and spirituality movements which cultivate lively contacts with the young acquire a particular importance. Movements, groups and associations working in the parochial environment must endeavour to construct a parish that may be a 'communion of communities'. These groups constitute significant faith experiences, stimulate conversion, awaken a sense of God and initiate persons into a life of prayer and apostolic spirit. A number of religious and priestly vocations come through these movements and they have proved their worth as ways of securing the future of the Church.

Parents and Family

51.　While nowadays some candidates do not give serious consideration to a vocation at the end of second-level education, 'long experience shows, a priestly vocation tends to show itself in the preadolescent years or in the earliest years of youth'.[120] The early support of a priestly calling is especially important in order to foster vocations in the Christian community. The good Catholic home has always been and will continue to be the seed of vocations to the priesthood and religious life.[121] The Second Vatican Council recognises the family's specific mission to education in the field of consecrated vocations: 'Children should be so educated that as adults they can with a mature sense of responsibility, follow their vocation, including a religious one, and choose their state of life.'[122] The family, a community of faith, life and love, is the normal place for the human, Christian and vocational growth of children. The educational mission of the family includes the whole complex of the educative sphere. Furthermore, a good

---

[118] IVT 28
[119] *Come Follow Me*, p. 14
[120] PDV 63

[121] PCV 39; *Handing on the Faith in the Home*, Irish Bishops' Pastoral (1994)
[122] GS 52; cf. FC 53

general education gives young people a better grounding for the same Christian education.[123]

52.   As the Irish bishops say in *Come Follow Me*, 'no matter how strong the peer or cultural pressures, it seems true that the most formative influence on the values of children is their parents ... In the past there were instances of young people being over-encouraged to enter seminaries and religious congregations. We know that in Ireland we had what was called 'the mother's or father's vocation'. But maybe the opposite is happening now. Vocations to the priesthood and religious life are often discouraged by parents and huge obstacles are put in the way of young people thinking of this way of life. We pray that you encourage generosity, love and a desire to service in your children. There are sacrifices for parents in the vocations of their children: their sons or daughters take on a way of life often not understood in the family. Parents themselves will miss the joy of grandchildren. But they will have the joy of knowing that the faith which they shared with their children has grown strongly and will help the lives of so many others in the spreading of the gospel of Jesus Christ both in Ireland and other parts of the world.'[124] They should continue to help those who seem to show the initial signs of a vocation to recognise this vocation more easily and to respond to it.

Schools and Teachers

53.   Teachers also should encourage all their students by word and example to live up to their Baptism and to grow in Christian maturity.[125] 'The time has come to speak courageously about priestly life as a priceless gift and a splendid and privileged form of Christian living. Educators, and priests in particular, should not be afraid to set forth explicitly and forcefully the priestly vocation as a real possibility for those young people who demonstrate the necessary gifts and talents.'[126]

54.   Colleges and schools which form part of the State post-primary school system have been faithful nurseries of vocations in the past.[127] The Catholic school, for its part, cultivates a profound Christian vision of the world; it

---

[123] FC 49
[124] *Come Follow Me*, p. 13
[125] PCV 45

[126] PDV 39; cf. 34–41
[127] PDV 63–64

promotes an integral approach to culture and education which, inspired by faith, helps to create an atmosphere inspired by the values of the Gospel. Even if this is not the ethos of a school, teachers committed to their faith can create the atmosphere where vocations thrive.

A Diocesan Vocations Organisation

55.   Because it is important for the whole Christian community to further this work of fostering vocations, in every diocese a Vocations Organisation should be established and built up.[128] The combined efforts of priests and religious, parents and teachers, should be fully utilised in this important work. In these organisations, the importance of engaging the young people themselves so that they may be the primary evangelisers of other young people[129] should be recognised.

56.   While the work of such a Vocations Organisation may be co-ordinated by one person, 'nowadays, there is an urgent need to move from a pastoral vocations programme run by one person to a pastoral programme more and more conceived as a community action'.[130] In this way, under the guidance of the Holy Spirit, the combined efforts of all – bishop, priests, religious, parents, teachers, apostolic societies (such as the St Joseph's Young Priests Society), young people themselves – may give rise to a renewed sense of Church and of the value of a life of service to the Church in the ministerial priesthood.

57.   The one charged by the bishop to co-ordinate the Vocations Organisation in the diocese should be carefully selected and given suitable training and support for this ministry. Taking into account the circumstances in which a person today may be discerning a call to priesthood, the ministry of vocations promotion needs someone capable of animating a team and collaborating with others involved in the process of discernment. It requires someone with the requisite skills for assessing and accompanying individuals in their discernment, someone who retains joy, confidence and a sense of mission, however many or few present themselves for labour in the Lord's harvest.

---

[128] OT 2; PO 11; Vatican II, Decree on the Adaptation and Renewal of Religious Life *Perfectae caritatis* (28 October 1965) 24; Second Vatican Council, Decree on the Pastoral Office of Bishops in the Church, *Christus Dominus*, 15; AG 16, 39; PCV 57–58
[129] PCV 4
[130] IVT 26

58.   In all prayer and work for the promotion of vocations, the needs of the whole People of God must be borne in mind. 'The work of fostering vocations should be done generously. It should cross the boundaries of individual dioceses, countries, religious congregations and rites and with the needs of the universal Church in view, should assist especially those areas for which workers are required with special urgency for the Lord's vineyard.'[131] The efforts of those engaged in every phase of this work should be marked by co-operation rather than competition. A coherent national approach to the promotion of vocations and the admission of candidates should be developed.

Discerning Vocations

59.   'No one has a *right* to receive the sacrament of Holy Orders. Indeed no one claims this office for himself; he is called to it by God. Anyone who thinks he recognizes the signs of God's call to the ordained ministry must humbly submit his desire to the authority of the Church, who has the responsibility and right to call someone to receive orders.'[132] The ministerial priesthood is God's free gift. Because not everyone who contemplates becoming a priest has a vocation, the Church has always placed a special emphasis on vocational discernment. This discernment is an expression of the Church's respect for every prospective candidate. It is out of respect for him that he should only be admitted to a seminary if there are clear signs that he is being called. The Church must therefore reflect at length over every application for seminary in order to establish whether or not the applicant has been truly chosen by God. As a guiding principle the bishop should do everything in his power to ensure that an intolerable burden is not placed on the shoulders of somebody ill-equipped personally or psychologically to bear it.

60.   As the Council says, 'Each candidate should be subjected to vigilant and careful inquiry, keeping in mind his age and development, concerning his right intention and freedom of choice, his spiritual, moral and intellectual fitness, adequate physical and mental health and possible hereditary traits. Account should also be taken of the candidate's capacity for understanding the obligations of the priesthood and carrying out his pastoral duties.'[133]

---

[131] OT 2
[132] CCC 2121
[133] OT 6

61.   Assisting the candidate in discerning his motivation or intention is important and should be carried out over a significant period of time by the vocations director. In the long run this will help both the applicant and the formation staff of the seminary in that the candidate can benefit to the fullest advantage from what is offered in the seminary programme. Due regard should be paid to the norms of professional confidentiality. His parish priest should be consulted about the candidate and his family background. The observations of the community should also be listened to. The law of the Church states: 'Christ's faithful are bound to reveal, before ordination, to the Ordinary or to the parish priest, such impediments to sacred orders as they may know about.'[134]

62.   This initial assessment is primarily concerned with suitability to start a formation programme and the candidates' potential to develop during the programme. It is of special importance for them to be able to express their vision of Jesus Christ, the Church and the priesthood. It is equally important for them to have the experience of prayer and to be able to say how they became aware of a call to the priesthood.

Accompanying the Candidate

63.   It is necessary that the vocations director or other trusted priest should get to know the candidate, establish a rapport with him and in time introduce him to the bishop. The vocations director should ask the candidate to write an autobiographical sketch giving some information on his family background, educational record, work experience, interests and personality. The vocations director's role will subsequently be one of prayerful and discerning accompaniment. This accompaniment in the external forum will be further enhanced by the candidate having a spiritual director appointed by the bishop to accompany him in the internal forum.

64.   It will also be of great help therefore to know something of the applicant's family background, his upbringing and education, his spiritual and human journey and the steps which have brought him to this important stage of his life and his physical and mental health. To this end testimony from a variety of

---

[134] CIC 104

trusted sources including parish priests, teachers, former employers, family members and family doctors can be valuable. This manner of pre-selection discernment is often necessary in order to ensure that the candidate is sufficiently healthy to withstand the significant demands of seminary life and subsequent ministry.

65.   Applicants must give some evidence of an overall personal balance, moral character and proper motivation.[135] This includes the requisite human, moral, spiritual, intellectual, physical, and psychological qualities for priestly ministry.[136]

66.   Diocesan bishops, religious ordinaries, vocations directors and seminaries should recognise that additional time will be necessary to prepare candidates without previous seminary formation for entrance into a four-year theology programme, preceded by a two-year philosophy programme.[137]

67.   Careful attention should be given especially to applicants who are recent converts to the Catholic faith. It is advisable that at least two or three years pass between their entry into the Church and their acceptance into a seminary programme. A suitable period of time should pass before entrance to the seminary in cases of Catholics in whom a recent conversion experience seems to precipitate a priestly vocation. Likewise, those who return to the practice of the faith after an extended period should not enter the seminary directly.

68.   A propaedeutic or foundation period of at least a year dedicated to the human, spiritual and intellectual preparation of aspirants for the major seminary as proposed by *Pastores dabo vobis* is essential for the formation of seminarians in Ireland today.[138] This Propaedeutic Year, should address the four headings of Formation as outlined by *Pastores dabo vobis*, while acknowledging the special needs of candidates entering seminary for diocesan priesthood in today's world. Its aim is to build upon the period of accompaniment which the candidate has already experienced. It should also help the candidate grow, whatever his age and experience, in knowledge and experience and in the knowledge of God and self, which is necessary if he is to be an effective minister. The Propaedeutic Year must take cognisance of the considerable discrepancy between the foregoing

---

[135] Pope John Paul II examines a central
motivational factor in relation to vocation; cf.
Redemptionis donum (1981), 7; cf. also
Congregation for Catholic Education, *Spiritual
Formation in Seminaries* (1979) 3

[136] CIC 241 § 1
[137] CIC 250
[138] Cf: PDV 62

style of life of candidates and the style of life expected of them in seminary.[139] It will gradually introduce him to what it means to be a priest in today's world and address any spiritual, cultural and human lacunae in his education and upbringing. It should also seek to address the particular needs of the older candidate. The methodology should enable the candidate to reflect on his own experience in light of the subject matter being presented.

69.   The primary aim of the human formation component of the course is to help the individual to begin the process of understanding and appreciating how God has shaped his individuality. Some basic input on human development is necessary, to bring about a fuller understanding of the human person. This will include a module on emotional and sexual development, which will give a foundation for obedience and celibacy. The course should help the individual to reflect on his life story, to appreciate his God-given strengths and come to an awareness of anything that might prevent him from making a free response to God's call, for example fears, anger, anxieties, poor self-image etc. Modules on time management, study skills, reading and writing skills, and information technology should be also available. The spiritual component should entail some basic input and help on how to pray so that prayer links with life and the aspirant's process of discernment. This may involve some praying and sharing in small groups. There must also be the opportunity for individual spiritual direction. Guidance should be given too on spiritual reading and time is to be set aside for quiet days and days of reflection. Ways of praying including *Lectio Divina* and praying with Scripture and Psalms should be explored. The intellectual component should provide a basic introduction to Scripture, Faith and Worship, Faith and Culture, the Liturgy and the Moral Life. Provision for a modest introduction to pastoral formation, including preparation, placements and an opportunity for reflection should also be made.

Admission to Seminary

70.   Today more than ever a compelling case exists for a co-ordinated approach to seminary assessment and admissions. 'The selection of candidates for priesthood and religious life needs to be an integral process involving the vocations director, interview board and the bishop or religious superior.'[140]

---

[139] The Propaedeutic Period – Congregation for Catholic Education (1998) 3

[140] *Child Sexual Abuse: Framework for a Church Response*, Irish Bishops' Conference (1996)

71.   Thus, it is essential to put into practice a judicious selection process that will foster both the individual candidate's growth and the good of the Church.[141] The Irish Bishops' Conference in their *Enquiries and Applications for Admission into Formation for Diocesan Priesthood*[142] document, set out a list of useful criteria, as part of a selection process, in bringing to light an individual's strengths and weaknesses so as to carry out a thorough assessment of these and to offer him a suitable programme of formation that will meet his needs.

72.   Clearly it is the bishop or religious superior who ultimately decides whether prospective candidates are to be recommended to seminary. He should endeavour to identify in them the presence of the requisite qualities or at least their true potential for growth. He should not admit to seminary candidates where those qualities or their true potential to flourish are missing. It will therefore prove helpful and indeed necessary for the candidate to meet the bishop and experience the interest of the bishop in his vocational story. The bishop should duly receive reports from the vocations director and the assessment panel as well as reports from parish priest, medical doctor, school and previous employers, before deciding whether the candidate should be recommended to seminary. He will also consider any psychological reports on the candidate.

73.   Many dioceses have found it helpful to enlist the aid of a group of suitably qualified people who would in turn serve on the diocesan assessment panel. The panel is chosen from people with relevant backgrounds, education, counselling, personnel management, medical qualifications and understanding of priesthood and religious life. It is desirable that they represent the different states of life and include both men and women, as in this way they remind the candidate that 'ordained ministers exercise their service for the entire people of God'.[143]

74.   It will also be important to establish the extent of the applicant's intellectual capabilities. Although not all candidates will be especially gifted academically, it is imperative for each individual to have the capacity to undertake 'the same human and scientific formation which prepares peers in the region for higher studies'.[144] As well as his capacity for intellectual growth, the

---

[141] CIC 241 § 1
[142] Approved 2002 – cf. Appendix 1

[143] CCC 1592
[144] CIC 234 and RF 16

prospective seminarian must also be capable of sustained human, spiritual, pastoral and moral growth. In other words, he must have certain verifiable qualities: 'a right intention, a sufficient degree of human maturity, a sufficiently broad knowledge of the doctrine of the faith, some introduction to methods of prayer and behaviour in conformity to Christian tradition'.[145] This entails, among other things, the ability to work and collaborate with others and to cultivate habits of prayer and research aimed at reinforcing the spiritual life, together with a sincerity of purpose and the absence of canonical impediment.[146]

75.   A psychological assessment may help both the candidate and the bishop to make an informed decision in each case. Thus, the Church holds that 'if necessary, the health, disposition and maturity of the candidate are to be established by experts'.[147] This assessment is not meant merely to be a form of 'screening', but should, in addition, furnish both candidate and bishop with a list of the candidate's qualities, capacities and talents. It is desirable that prior contact with the psychologist or medical doctor be made in order to clarify what kind of assessment is being sought and its purpose. 'The first thing is to help the students seriously and sincerely to ponder before God whether they can really believe themselves called to the priesthood, and make them able to sort out the motives of their intention.'[148] It is thus useful if the psychologist or medical doctor and diocesan authorities have already established a working relationship and agreed upon a set of key areas to be assessed.

76.   Dioceses should provide guidelines for psychologists and for others involved in the admission process, describing objectively those traits and attitudes which give hope of a true vocation as well as those characteristics which indicate that a priestly vocation is not present. Those employed in the psychological evaluation of seminarians should be well versed in and supportive of the Church's expectations of candidates for the priesthood, especially in regard to celibacy. Examples of the kind of subjects to be covered are: interpersonal relationships, leadership qualities, decision-making ability, personal identity, sexual identity, emotional stability, interests and hobbies, motivation for priesthood and family background.

---

[145] PDV 62
[146] Cf. CIC 1040–1043 and RF 39

[147] CIC 642
[148] RF 39

77.   The candidate should be prepared for the assessment and apprised of its purpose and time-frame, the names of those who will receive a report of the assessment (usually the candidate, the bishop and the seminary) and the consent he needs to give before the assessment proceeds. A candidate's willingness to undergo this assessment is a sign of his 'willingness to submit his desire to the authority of the Church, which has the responsibility and right to call someone to receive orders'.[149]

78.   Regarding the results of psychological testing and other confidential materials, the bishop should observe closely all legal requirements and utilise appropriate release forms.[150] Throughout the admission process, the candidate's right to privacy should be respected and the careful management of confidential materials observed.

79.   In the admission procedure, the life experience the candidate brings to the seminary should be openly and forthrightly discussed. The seminarian's level of insight and motivation to address areas such as interpersonal relations and psychosexual development are important criteria for admission. The process should look for signs of self-acceptance and self-esteem and uncover his attitude and behaviour towards authority. The candidate should also demonstrate that he can persevere in the pursuit of an objective. Admission of some candidates should be delayed until these personal issues are better identified or resolved.

80.   Attention should be given to the family background of all applicants. Those from particularly dysfunctional families require careful evaluation before admission. The applicant's willingness to address family and personal issues should be determined prior to admission. In those instances when long-term therapeutic intervention may be needed, it should be completed before the candidate enters a programme of priestly formation. If these issues are serious, the candidate's application may have to be refused.

81.   The number of applications from older candidates is increasing. Many of them have completed third-level studies and often some years of work in areas other than theological education or pastoral ministry. Others may have

---

[149] CCC 1578; cf. CIC 1029   [150] CIC 220

interrupted their secondary education and will require assistance in reaching a suitable standard. Bringing a varied background to the seminary, they represent an asset to the seminary programme and to the Church, though at times, their backgrounds can involve complicated personal or professional situations. While admission procedures should be sensitive to their situation, they must be no less thorough. In the case of applicants who are middle-aged or older, there are particular vulnerability factors that need to be looked out for when discerning the suitability of a candidate, such as substance abuse, unresolved sexual identity, instability at college or work, hostility or violence manifested towards others, dependency and the need to impose his way of thinking upon others.

82. Where applicants have already been in a seminary or formation programme, dioceses, seminaries, religious institutes or societies have a serious duty to investigate the causes of the departure from any previous institution. The candidate too should release all relevant information concerning their departure from any previous programme of priestly formation. If such records indicate difficulties, the diocese or the institution should prudently weigh admission, making sure that problems have been overcome and positive growth has taken place. Particular attention should be paid to the presence of hereditary defects, problems concerning human and affective maturity, psychological and sexual anomalies and ideological and doctrinal difficulties. In cases of doubt, the benefit given should be in favour of the Church lest the suggestion of disparity of selection criteria alter the climate of fraternal collegiality and trust.[151]

83. An especially careful investigation must be made by the Ordinary before accepting seminary students who have been dismissed or who seek transfer from another seminary. It is also required that the consultation take place between the administrations of both seminaries with the necessary documentation about the applicants' previous records being provided. This must be done in every instance. Similar criteria must be applied to applicants who have been in religious formation programmes and who are now applying to a diocesan seminary.[152] Moreover, rectors should keep in mind that 'the problem concerns not only expelled seminarians, but also those who withdrew voluntarily, given that such withdrawal at times happens in order to avoid a formal expulsion'.[153]

---

[151] Congregation for Catholic Education, *Instruction to the Episcopal Conferences on the Admission to Seminary of Candidates Coming From Other Seminaries or Religious Families* (8 March 1996)

[152] Ibid.

[153] Ibid.; cf. CIC 241 § 3

84.   Applicants for the priesthood whose marriages have been annulled should be scrutinised carefully. While these men may have canonical freedom it is important to ascertain if and how previous obstacles to a marriage commitment would affect their viability as candidates for the priesthood. Addressing the topic in 1983 the Congregation for Catholic Education wrote to the United States Episcopal Conference as follows: 'Usually in the cases brought to our attention, the men have been admitted as candidates in dioceses where their former marriages are not known, financial matters pertaining to the marriages have been settled and, especially, the needs of any children of such marriages properly secured.

'When a marriage is annulled on the grounds of "psychological incompetence" on the part of the man, though, serious questions are raised if he should present himself as a candidate for Holy Orders. In affirmation of the principle that the degree of maturity and "psychological competence" required for the Sacrament of Holy Orders is no less than that required for the Sacrament of Marriage, we would respectfully advise that particular care be taken in such cases.

'In some instances, bishops have asked for a psychological assessment of a candidate before accepting him. Whilst acknowledging that real Christian growth and maturity may have taken place, we would point out the paradox – with its dangers to the sanctity of the Sacraments and the integrity of Tribunals – of a psychological assessment for admission to seminary which stands in apparent contradiction to that undertaken earlier for the Tribunal, on the basis of which the Decree of Nullity was issued.'[154]

Points Regarding the Seminary Programme

85.   Seminaries sponsoring courses of priestly formation that abbreviate the requirements of canon 250 need the explicit permission of the Congregation for Catholic Education to offer such programmes.

86.   Because seminarians today come from a variety of academic, cultural, personal and spiritual situations and have different abilities, admission to the formation programme must be carefully considered. A preparatory programme should take into consideration both the needs of these applicants and the special gifts they bring to the formation process because of their previous education and experience.

---

[154] Congregation for Catholic Education, Letter to
    the United States Episcopal Conference, 1983

Chapter III

THE SEMINARY

87.   The Seminary is more than a material space; it is first of all a spiritual place. 'The seminary … should be a spiritual place, a way of life, an atmosphere that fosters and ensures a process of formation, so that the person who is called to the priesthood by God may become, with the Sacrament of Orders, a living image of Jesus Christ, Head and Shepherd of the Church.'[155] After calling his disciples and before sending them out, indeed in order to be able to send them out to preach the gospel, Jesus asks them to set aside a certain time 'to be with him'.[156] 'In its deepest identity, the seminary is called to be in its own way *a continuation of the Church of the Apostolic community gathered about Jesus.*'[157] First and foremost the mission of the seminary is to help students to live in the company of Jesus, as the apostles did, developing a close intimate relationship with him, so that they will be able to act and speak in his name, *in persona Christi.* 'To live in the seminary which is a school of the gospel, means to follow Christ as the apostles did.'[158] 'The seminary can be seen as a place and a period of life. But it is above all, *an educational community in progress*: It is a community established by the bishops to offer to those called by the Lord to serve as apostles the possibility of re-living the experience of formation which Our Lord provided for the Twelve.'[159]

88.   Seminaries therefore are necessary for the formation of priests.[160] The 1990 Synod on the Formation of Priests proposed: 'The institution of the Major Seminary, as the best place for formation, is to be certainly reaffirmed as the normal place, in the material sense as well, for a community and hierarchical life, indeed as the proper home for the formation of candidates for the priesthood, with superiors who are truly dedicated to this service. The institution has

---

[155] PDV 42
[156] Cf. Mk 3:13–15
[157] PDV 60
[158] Message of the Synod Fathers (28 October 1990)
[159] PDV 60
[160] Cf. OT 4; PDV 60

produced many good results down the ages and continues to do so all over the world.'[161] That said, it has also to be acknowledged that the work of the seminary and the programme of formation it offers require continuous renewal.[162]

89.   The seminary is not to be seen simply as a place to live and study. It is desirable that it be experienced as 'a community built on deep friendship and charity, so that it can be considered a true family living in joy'.[163] Its joy and strength spring from the celebration of the Liturgy. It is moulded daily through reading and meditation on the word of God. It is imbued with a strong sense of brotherly love and a genuine desire to make more real in the world Christ's kingdom of truth and justice, love and peace. It is 'a community committed to formation, the human, spiritual, intellectual and pastoral formation of future priests'.[164] 'As an ecclesial community ... the seminary should nourish the meaning of communion between the candidates and their bishop and presbyterate in such a way that they share in their hopes and anxieties and learn to extend this openness to the needs of the universal Church.'[165]

90.   Formation in the spirit and service of communion is brought about specifically through experience of the common life. This is one of the essential elements of formation. It helps the student to be more outgoing and generous. It helps him overcome attitudes centred on himself and the predominant pursuit of selective groups. It is necessary that candidates be formed in a relationship of close collaboration and deep fraternal union between diocesan and religious clergy.

91.   The community life in the seminary should prepare candidates for the priesthood so that in the end, raised to Holy Orders, they may be united with the wider community of the diocesan presbyterate.[166] The community life of the seminary can be valuable in helping students to learn to work as part of a presbyteral team in communion with the bishop. Despite an increase in collaboration and the sense of the presbyterium among priests, many priests live on their own and may experience considerable loneliness. Community life in a seminary should not prevent students from developing the resources they will need to live this reality. It is hoped that the emphasis on preparation for the

---

[161] *Propositio* 20 quoted in PDV 60
[162] Cf. PDV 61
[163] PDV 60

[164] PDV 61
[165] *Propositio* 20 quoted in PDV 60
[166] RF 47

collaborative exercise of ministry will help priests both to work as members of a team and to be able to deal with the problems of loneliness.

92.   Seminary formation helps seminarians to 'acquire a tranquil, convinced and free choice of the grave responsibilities which (they) must assume in conscience before God and the Church'[167] and to acquire the personal skills that will enable them to live a celibate life as the Church envisages it,[168] so that they may, with undivided hearts, dedicate themselves to the service of the Lord and of his Body, the Church. Thus, the purpose of formation is to clarify and deepen the initial choice a candidate has made so that it leads to a more responsible, free and conscious response.[169] This entails a growth in freedom, which is essential to vocation and is necessary for a true dialogue with the Lord who calls.[170]

93.   To achieve its purpose a seminary needs a sufficient number of students to guarantee effective educational programmes and a balanced formational community. Steps should be taken to avoid unnecessary duplication of effort and dissipation of resources. Brotherly collaboration between seminaries, diocesan and religious should therefore be encouraged.[171]

94.   Through the formation programme offered by the seminary a student is encouraged to grow, to mature and to develop so that he may become more like Christ, Shepherd, Teacher and Priest for the service of the whole people of God. Such growth demands discipline and the exercise of responsibility on the part of the student and the seminary strives to provide an atmosphere where this is possible.

95.   In every seminary therefore there must be a Rule approved by the Bishops' Conference in which are set out the important points of discipline affecting the students' daily life and the order of the whole institution.[172]

96.   The common life serves to unite not only persons but charisms and various functions. It also leads towards obedience and detachment from one's own will. A rule directs seminary life, for the common life demands discipline. In this way a man learns discipline in his life and the proper occupation of his time and

---

[167] Pope Paul IV, Encyclical Letter *Sacerdotalis coelibatus* (24 June 1967), 69
[168] OT 4
[169] PDV 25, 42
[170] PDV 36
[171] OT 7; DMR 30b, 55
[172] CIC 243

energies. This helps him to achieve a self-control which is needed to give himself entirely to a task and to others. It is the human basis for an obedience lived in union with the obedience of Christ.

97.   Obedience does not exclude the exercise of responsibility because discipline must be understood in a climate of confidence and mutual respect between seminarians and their formators. Candidates must work actively and conscientiously in their own formation and structures of responsibility must permit them to participate in areas of responsibility in seminary life. Obedience includes participation in decision making. This participation initiates students into the process of pastoral decision making, which includes listening, collaboration and sharing of responsibility. However, ultimately a seminarian must comply with the lawful decisions of his superior.

98.   Each student should generously and willingly observe the regulations laid down in the Rule or in other decisions taken by the rector and the formation staff, realising how necessary this is for community life as well as for his own personal formation. If discipline is to be effective in his formation, it must be accepted from personal conviction and supernatural motivation.

99.   As he progresses through the seminary and as his maturity increases, the rules of discipline should gradually be lessened so that the student may learn to act out of deep conviction and to use his freedom with discretion.[173]

100.   Candidates entering seminaries are increasingly diverse in age, experience and faith development. Because candidates come from a variety of backgrounds and have mixed talents and abilities, formation programmes should strive for flexibility in order to meet students' needs. Programmes also should strive to be thorough and comprehensive in the education they provide. In this regard most, if not all, prospective seminarians should complete a Propaedeutic Year.[174]

101.   The formation programme not only prepares students in philosophy and theology[175] but also brings to maturity their understanding of the faith, assisting them to develop a spirituality consistent with a priestly vocation. Accordingly,

[173] OT 11
[174] Cf. PDV 62
[175] CIC 250. 'Philosophical and theological studies which are conducted in the seminary itself can be pursued successively or conjointly in accord with the programme of priestly formation; these studies are to encompass a period of at least six full years in such a way that two full years are devoted to the philosophical disciplines and four full years to theological studies.'

daily Eucharist, the Liturgy of the Hours, sacramental reconciliation, community and personal prayer, spiritual direction, conferences by formation personnel, days of recollection and retreats, devotion to Our Lady, intellectual and pastoral formation and community life are essential components of the seminary formation.

102. In some cases it may not be possible for a seminary to provide all the elements of a formation programme from its own resources. In such instances it will be necessary to adopt a collaborative approach to formation, where the seminary provides a major part of the programme, while other dimensions, such as the academic, may be availed of in another institution.

103. In the collaborative approach, it is the responsibility of the seminary to ensure the integration of the various components of the programme. The goals of the seminary in the area of philosophy and undergraduate theology should also be closely monitored and the legitimate rights of Ordinaries should be recognised.

104. When the seminary, university and house of formation are interrelated, care should be taken that the various components of the programme are integrated in a careful and comprehensive manner so that each institution has a clear understanding of its specific responsibilities. It is essential that all parties in such a collaborative effort understand the specialised and pastoral nature of priestly formation.

105. The purpose of the theology programme is the proximate preparation of candidates for the priesthood. Seminarians presented for ordination should be converted to the service of Christ, understand the tradition of the Church and possess the attitudes and skills necessary to begin priestly ministry. They should also desire to grow in the spiritual life, in theological knowledge and in ministerial expertise after ordination. In the pursuit of this mission, the theology programme unites human, spiritual, intellectual and pastoral formation into an integral programme of priestly formation.

106. For this reason, every seminary should incorporate as an essential part of its mission statement a brief summary of the Church's doctrinal understanding of the ministerial priesthood, keeping before its eyes its fundamental purpose. Such a statement should indicate that the ministerial priesthood differs in essence from

the priesthood of all the baptised. 'Priests by the anointing of the Holy Spirit are signed with a special character and so are configured to Christ the priest in such a way that they are able to act in the person of Christ the head.'[176] 'In the person of Christ' the priest 'effects the Eucharistic sacrifice and offers it to God in the name of all the people'.[177] The configurement to Christ in the sacrament of orders confers a special participation in the Lord's mission to teach, sanctify and lead.

107.   The seminary has specific responsibilities to the dioceses that sponsor it and to those which it serves. Indeed, relationships between seminary and dioceses are a source of mutual enrichment and support.

108.   The statutes of all seminaries and ecclesiastical faculties should be in accord with Canon Law and all legislation governing seminary and theological formation.

STUDENTS

109.   Since the principal agent of priestly formation is the Holy Spirit the seminarian must therefore understand his formation journey as collaboration with Him. He must strive to render himself more open to the formative power of the Holy Spirit 'who dispenses his gifts in variety … according to his wealth and the requirements of the ministries'.[178]

110.   From the outset the student must also be aware that he is the person most responsible for his own formation: 'we must not forget that the candidate is a necessary and irreplaceable agent in his own formation. No one can replace us in the responsible freedom that we have as individual persons'.[179] In this regard, the student shall fully engage in all aspects of the formation programme.

111.   The student should be open, honest and mature with his formators and teachers.

---

[176] PO 2; LG 21, 18, 29
[177] LG 10

[178] Cf. RF 5 and 1 Cor 12:1–11
[179] PDV 69

112.   The onus is on the student to satisfy the formation personnel that he is preparing himself appropriately for priesthood and that he is a suitable candidate for Orders. However, each student must realise from the outset of his formation that there is no right to Ordination.[180]

113.   The student body should strive at all times to create a spirit of fraternity, which helps to stimulate each one in his effort to form himself. Each student should do his part to create an environment of joy, harmony, respect, mutual support, openness, responsibility and common ideals.

114.   Assessment of the student should continue during the course of his studies so that there may be reasonable certainty about his vocation. The student should be encouraged to arrive at a deep self-knowledge and appropriate help and guidance should be available to him in this task so that his 'definitive choice of a state of life should be made in good time'.[181]

115.   A written report should be furnished regularly by the Seminary authorities to the Ordinary. The report should seek to evaluate the student's intelligence, maturity, skill, moral character and aptitude for ministry and for a life of celibacy.

116.   The seminary authorities should remain in close contact with the diocese or congregation so that an evaluation of the student's progress during the summer vacation may also be obtained.

117.   The *scrutinia* prescribed by Canon Law before taking Orders should be made with special care so that a prudent judgement about the seminarian's suitability may be made. The formation staff should, with the help of parish priests, selected lay people and respected sources, strive to put together an accurate picture of the student and make this available to the Ordinary.[182]

118.   Additionally, students should have the opportunity at specific stages of their formation journey to avail of a specific period set aside for extended prayer and reflection on the priestly vocation.[183]

---

[180] Cf. CCC 1578; OT 6
[181] RF 40
[182] CIC 1051, 1052 and RF 41
[183] RF 42a

119. Students should also have the opportunity for an initial period of reflection, prayer and study at the outset of their formation which would have as its primary focus an introduction to the mystery of Christ and the history of salvation.[184]

120. Under the direction of a competent supervisor, students should be encouraged to assimilate their pastoral training by assisting in parishes or other suitable pastoral assignments according to the clearly defined terms of reference set down by their seminary.

121. The vacation periods constitute a significant proportion of the seminary year and contribute to the formation of seminarians. During these periods they should grow in their appreciation of the priesthood through contact with the priests of their own parish and diocese. They should also come to a deeper awareness of the daily lives of men and women as they follow their Christian vocation. The vacation periods also provide an opportunity to grow in awareness of the world-wide Church and to develop language skills which might be of use in future ministry.

122. During the vacation periods they should strive to live their personal faith in whatever circumstances they find themselves and be devoted to personal prayer and the sacraments, especially the Eucharist. They should give good example to those they meet and refrain from any behaviour that would endanger their vocation or give scandal.

123. During the summer vacation they shall accept such pastoral work as may be allocated to them by their Ordinary. In particular, all those studying theology should be assigned to a pastoral placement of at least three weeks duration.

124. In cases where there may be a doubt about the student's vocation or his readiness for Orders it may be prudent for him to spend a specified period of time working or studying under suitable guidance, with access to spiritual direction and counselling, away from the seminary.

125. Students who are unsuited to the priesthood should be kindly and candidly helped to recognise this fact and, where possible, assisted in choosing another state of life.[185]

---

[184] RF 41   [185] RF 40

CONTINUING EVALUATION OF SEMINARIANS

126. Education and growth are gradual processes. Hence the continuing evaluation of students is necessary. Seminarians profit most from a system of regular evaluation in which they receive clear and accurate information about their behaviour and attitudes so that they can address what is inappropriate and develop in those areas in which they may be weak. Such evaluation is primarily the responsibility of the seminary formation staff. The formation staff should also involve the seminarians themselves, their teachers, their various supervisors and others involved in their human, spiritual, intellectual and pastoral formation.

127. The regular review of a student's progress should be done in a constructive way. The seminary should have a written statement of the criteria used in evaluating students and their suitability for ministries and Orders. Vocational growth assessment and counselling may be employed if it is considered helpful in this regard.

128. The attitude with which evaluation is approached is vital to its effectiveness. Both staff and students should approach the process in a spirit of mutual trust and confidence, relating to each other in healthy, positive ways.

129. 'The candidate himself is a necessary and irreplaceable agent in his own formation.'[186] This is nowhere more true than in his responsibility for forming his own character.

130. The seminary should require an evaluation of seminarians' summer activities from the appropriate diocesan personnel. This report should evaluate their pastoral activities and their fidelity to spiritual exercises.

131. The Ordinary expects the objective and critical judgement of the seminary rector and formation staff in coming to the decision to call seminarians to Orders. A recommendation to the Ordinary should reflect a clear consensus of

---

[186] PDV 69

those who have been involved with a seminarian's training and formation. Those responsible should regard the matter of evaluation as their most important task. In all evaluative processes, they should keep clearly in mind the goal of seminary formation, namely ordination to the priesthood for ministry to the people of God.

132. A statement, at least once a year, to the Ordinary, should provide a clear estimation of the student's human, spiritual, intellectual and pastoral progress, based on his behaviour, attitudes, academic performance and pastoral reports. The evaluation also should include an estimation of his capacity to lead a celibate life.

133. The report should state whether or not the candidate possesses sufficient intelligence, personal maturity, interpersonal skills, common sense, moral character and aptitude for ministry to continue in the seminary programme and finally to be ordained to the priesthood. Furthermore there should be accountability in the external forum for seminarians' participation in spiritual exercises of the seminary and their growth as men of faith. Seminarians should be accountable for simplicity of life, ability to assume responsibility and mature respect for church authority. Within the parameters of the external forum, habits of prayer and commitment to the spiritual life are also areas of accountability.[187]

134. Seminarians who lack the positive qualities for continuing in the seminary should not nourish unrealistic expectations with resultant damage either to themselves, fellow seminarians or the Church. If seminarians do not have the qualities that will allow them to work as priests in harmonious and effective ways, it is a matter of justice to individual seminarians and to the Church to communicate this to them as early as possible and in a constructive manner. In co-operation with the diocesan bishop, they should be advised to leave the seminary.

135. In a case where a negative evaluation seems to indicate that a seminarian should not continue in formation or should he not be recommended for ordination, a fair hearing should be given to the student's assessment of himself.

---

[187] Congregation for Divine Worship and the
   Discipline of the Sacraments, *Scrutinies*
   Regarding the Suitability of Candidates for Orders
   (28 November 1997)

136. In cases of doubt about the readiness of some students for advancement to orders or about their progress in achieving maturity, consideration can be given by the diocesan bishop to a period away from the seminary. The time period involved should be specified, not open-ended. Likewise, appropriate supervision is necessary so that leave of absence or deferral of orders can bring about needed growth. There should be regular contact between the supervisor and a member of the seminary formation staff. In such a situation, the burden of proof of readiness for orders rests with the seminarian and doubt is resolved in favour of the Church.

137. It is the responsibility of the Ordinary to make the final judgement on a student's fitness for admission to candidacy, institution in the ministries of reader and acolyte, and promotion to sacred orders.

138. In accordance with the norms of the Second Vatican Council, the Holy See and the Bishops' Conference, the Ordinary will look for certain qualities in candidates for sacred orders. Candidates should possess a sense of the ministerial priesthood that is ecclesial as manifested by:

(a) Fidelity to the Word of God and to the teaching of the magisterium, combined with a deep love for the Church;

(b) Commitment to a life of personal prayer and the ability to assist others in their spiritual growth;

(c) Love for the sacramental life of the Church, especially the Eucharist and the sacrament of Reconciliation;

(d) Acceptance of a lifelong commitment to celibacy, obedience and simplicity of life;

(e) Sensitivity to the ecumenical dimension of the Church's mission;

(f) A commitment to service as manifested by:

- Ability to collaborate in ministry with the bishop, fellow priests and lay co-workers;

- Commitment to justice, peace and human life as well as to the universal mission of the Church;

- Pastoral skill and sensitivity in proclaiming God's Word and leading the people of God in prayer.

139. Candidates should also show evidence of having interiorised their seminary formation. Growth in self-awareness and sound personal identity are the hallmarks of a healthy personality, which establishes a secure basis for the spiritual life. Such growth may be demonstrated by:

(a)   Sound and prudent judgement;

(b)   Capacity for courageous and decisive leadership;

(c)   *Ability to establish and maintain wholesome friendships and to deal* with intimacy;

(d)   Ability to work in a collaborative, professional manner with men and women, foregoing personal preference in the interests of co-operative effort for the common good.[188]

140. With regard to the rite of Admission to Candidacy and the institution in the ministries of Reader and Acolyte, the directives of the apostolic letters *Ad pascendum* and *Ministeria quaedam*, the *Code of Canon Law*, the *Rites of Institution* and the *ratio fundamentalis* are to be followed, as well as the more specific directives of the Bishops' Conference.

141. Seminarians must be at least twenty years of age and have begun their theological studies before applying for the rite of Admission to Candidacy for sacred orders.[189]

142. Although the ministries are to be received by candidates for the priesthood, they are not simply steps toward ordination. No one is to be instituted as Reader

---

[188] Cf. PDV 43; CIC 245   [189] *Ad pascendum*, Norms, 1(b)

or Acolyte without a period of preparation in all aspects of the respective ministry. The canonical interval required between the ministry of acolyte and diaconate is to be observed.[190]

Formation and Administrative Staff

143. In each seminary there should be staff responsible for its direction. These will include the Rector, Vice-Rector, Director of Formation, Spiritual Director and other officers according to the traditions and needs of the seminary. According to the Decree *Optatam totius* 'seminary superiors and professors should be chosen from among the best'.[191] In some instances one member of staff may hold more than one office. 'The function, rights and duties of each and their just emoluments should also be clearly defined.'[192] Ultimately, however, 'the effectiveness of the training offered depends on the maturity and strength of personality of those entrusted with formation, from the human and the Gospel points of view'.[193]

144. The formation and administrative staff are to be appointed by the bishop or bishops and with due consultation, according to the statutes of the seminary. The essential qualities required include 'possessing a strong spirit of faith, an active priestly and pastoral consciousness, stability in one's vocation, a clear ecclesial sense, a skill for human relations and leadership, a mature psychological, emotional and affective equilibrium, intelligence united with prudence and wisdom, a true cultivation of the mind and heart, the capacity to collaborate, a profound knowledge of the mind of a young person and a community spirit.'[194] 'Besides the necessary natural and supernatural gifts, they should have according to their duties due spiritual, human, pastoral, professional and pedagogical training.'[195]

145. All members of the formation and administrative staff collaborate with the Rector and should be chosen with great care, since they are to be the Church's

---

[190] CIC 1035 § 2
[191] OT 14; cf. DPSE 23
[192] RF 27
[193] PDV 66
[194] DPSE 24
[195] RF 28

representatives before the students 'and should be men of deep priestly and apostolic spirit' capable of sustained fraternal collaboration and of fomenting a true sense of community.[196]

146.   After the Ordinary, the Rector of the seminary has a central and pivotal role and is principally responsible for formation,[197] for the spiritual and personal welfare of the seminary community and for co-ordinating the work of the staff in a harmonious and effective manner. He should also preside regularly at prayer and at Eucharist.

147.   The Rector is assisted in his work by the Vice-Rector, who fulfils his duties in his absence, and by other administrative officers as is customary or necessary.[198]

148.   The Director of Formation assists the Rector in overseeing the evaluation process and has a responsibility for the authentic intellectual, pastoral, human and spiritual formation in the external forum. He may not therefore act as a spiritual director or confessor to any student in the seminary where he works. The Director of Formation works actively for the integral formation of seminarians in his care.

149. The Spiritual Director is to guide wisely, from within a privileged relationship, the student's path of spiritual progress, by means of wise counsel, firm direction, generous encouragement and prayer.

150.   'The spiritual director, with his duty of offering to the community and to individuals, in the confidential relationship of spiritual direction, a sure guidance in the search for the will of God and in vocational discernment should refine his capacities to welcome, to listen, to converse and to understand, together with a good knowledge of spiritual theology, of the other theological disciplines and of the human and pedagogical sciences. No means should be spared to give him the possibility of attending an institute or at least an intensive course of spirituality.'[199]

---

[196] RF 70

[197] CIC 260

[198] RF 70

[199] DPSE 61

151. In virtue of their role in the internal forum spiritual directors may not participate in the evaluation of any seminarian. It should also be kept in mind that 'spiritual direction is an essentially theological and ecclesial fact, distinct from psychological therapy or assistance'.[200] In each seminary there is to be at least one spiritual director, though the students are also free to approach other priests who have been deputed to this work by the bishop.[201]

152. All the administrative and formation staff should take particular care to make adequate provision for appropriate and frequent dialogue with the students, with each other and with the Ordinary. They should strive to keep their skills and knowledge 'up to date through attendance at conferences or courses such as are held to review progress in spiritual or pedagogical sciences, or to learn about new methods and recent experience'.[202]

Academic Staff

153. The priest in his prophetic mission is called to be a teacher and the Master himself instructs his disciples to 'teach all nations',[203] and all those charged with the intellectual formation of seminarians should be dedicated to their total formation and to fostering within the seminary a genuine educational community.[204]

154. The professor or teacher 'using all the methods and techniques provided by his science, carries out his task at the mandate of the Church and co-operates with the bishop in his task of teaching'.[205]

155. All members of the academic staff are to be approved and appointed by the competent ecclesiastical authority on the recommendation of the rector and according to the approved statutes of the particular institute.[206] 'As a general rule teachers of the sacred subjects are to be priests.'[207]

---

[200] DPSE 61
[201] CIC 239 § 2
[202] RF 30
[203] Cf. Mt 28:19

[204] PDV 66 and RF 38
[205] PDV 67
[206] CIC 253 § 1
[207] RF 33

156. 'Bearing in mind (as the Synod Fathers have indeed done) the indications of the Exhortation *Christifideles laici* and of the Apostolic Letter *Mulieris dignitatem*, which stress the suitability of a healthy influence of lay spirituality and of the charism of femininity in every educational itinerary, it is worthwhile to involve, in ways that are prudent, the co-operation also of *lay faithful, both men and women*, in the work of training future priests. They are to be selected with care, within the framework of Church laws and according to their particular charisms and proven competence.'[208]

157. Personal faith, virtue and lifestyle, together with academic qualifications and teaching ability, prepare the teacher of Scripture for the formation of future ministers of the Word.[209]

158. All members of academic staff teach first by the quality of their lives. They are to exhibit a deep love of the Church and appreciation of the priesthood and a fraternal and collaborative spirit. 'A particular problem arises from the need to establish a good harmony between theological teaching and the formational policy of the seminary, with its vision of the priesthood and of the various questions concerning the life of the Church. This spirit of understanding, which must be continually strengthened in the institutes which have their own theological teaching staff, is even more necessary in those cases in which studies are carried out at theological faculties or in other institutes of theological studies. To such an end, 'the teacher of theology, like any other educator, should remain in communion and sincerely co-operate with all the other people who are involved in the formation of future priests and offer with scientific precision, generosity, humility and enthusiasm his own original and expert contribution.'[210]

159. A sufficient number of professors and teachers should be appointed, taking into account the subjects to be taught, the method of teaching and the number of students.[211]

160. It is important that the academic staff have sound academic qualifications and be competent in the art of teaching. Those who teach the sacred sciences and philosophy must hold at least a licentiate recognised by the Holy See. For other subjects, teachers should hold fitting academic qualifications.

---

[208] PDV 66
[209] EB 586
[210] DPSE, 32; cf. PDV 67
[211] RF 32

161. 'Where the faithful are involved in teaching in seminaries, it becomes necessary to provide for their appropriate religious and apostolic formation so that their work may be in complete conformity with the ends proper to priestly formation.'[212]

162. While always enjoying 'the freedom proper to theological research which is exercised within the Church's faith', the professor or teacher must strive not to 'forget that as a teacher he is not presenting his personal doctrines but ... the understanding of the faith ... in the name of the Lord and his Church'.[213]

163. Members of the teaching staff should hold regular scheduled meetings and should engage in regular review procedures and continuing evaluation programmes.

164. Professors and teachers should maintain professional competence in their disciplines. It is desirable that, so far as possible, they should do this through participation in professional associations, study leaves and sabbatical programmes and in ongoing study and research of their subject and of the art of teaching.

165. Professors and teachers should work in harmony with the administrative and formation staff, forming with them 'a single community of educators to present together with their students the genuine image of one family which fulfils the prayer of Our Lord "that they may be one"'.[214]

HUMAN FORMATION

166. Church documents since the Second Vatican Council recognise that the formation of candidates for the priesthood must address the areas of human, spiritual and priestly identity. Since these three identities are interrelated, the formation process cannot neglect any one of them. Of course, it is the theological

---

[212] Cf. Pope John Paul II, Apostolic Constitution *Sapientia christiana* (1979) on Ecclesiastical Universities and Faculties, and Norms of Application of the Sacred Congregation for Catholic Education for the Correct Implementation of the Apostolic Constitution *Sapientia christiana*
[213] Cf. PDV 67 and EVT 11–12
[214] Jn 17:11; cf. OT 5 and RF 38

identity of the priest that gives the candidate for the priesthood the context within which this commitment takes on meaning. A seminarian must never lose sight of the supernatural dimension of his vocation. It situates all of the human skills to be acquired upon a sound theological foundation in order to shape an identity that will allow the seminarian to commit himself at the core of his being.

167. A basic theological axiom is that grace builds on nature. Priestly formation demands both a clear theological vision of the priest's identity and a vision of the human person which can integrate all the dimensions of a priest's identity with a process of growth in which grace and freedom are at work. The call to holiness implies the surrender of the whole person in loving dialogue with God.[215] The purpose of seminary formation is to help candidates for the priesthood to 'acquire a tranquil, convinced and free choice of the grave responsibilities which they must assume in conscience before God and the Church',[216] and to acquire the personal skills that will enable them to live a celibate life as the Church envisages it. The goal of human formation is that a candidate, understanding himself and integrating his human nature and the gift of grace inherent in the call to priesthood, may be better prepared for the service of mission that will be his for the rest of life.

168. In the Apostolic Exhortation *Pastores dabo vobis* there is a fundamental insistence on human formation as the basis of all priestly formation. Priests are to be mature men. 'The whole work of priestly formation would be deprived of its necessary foundation if it lacked a suitable human formation.'[217] Moreover, 'the candidate himself is a necessary and irreplaceable agent in his own formation: all formation, priestly formation included, is ultimately a self-formation'.[218] For seminarians to become fully functioning, they must assume full responsibility for their lives, becoming the primary agents of their own formation in order to achieve human maturity and spiritual wholeness. The significance of personal growth, and its intimate connection with spiritual development, presumes and builds upon continuing theological growth and character development consistent with a vocation to the priesthood. On his educational journey, the community life of the seminary, the service and example of the staff and their professional collaborators, together with the seminarian's own family, provide the environment in which his personal growth and character development take place.

---

[215] *Pastores dabo vobis* states that 'the greater or lesser degree of the holiness of the minister has a real effect on the proclamation of the word, the celebration of the sacraments and the leadership of the community in charity', 25. In this is seen the relationship that exists between apostolic effectiveness and holiness
[216] *Sacerdotalis coelibatus* 69
[217] *Propositio* 21 quoted in PDV 43
[218] PDV 69

169. Candidates for the priesthood must be helped to live creatively with solitude enabling them to grow in affective maturity in order 'to bring to human relationships of serene friendship and deep brotherliness, a strong, lively and personal love for Jesus Christ'.[219] Today seminarians need a 'training in freedom' in the areas of interpersonal relations and affective maturity, especially celibacy.[220] This training in freedom helps the seminarian to know himself better and identify himself with the acts of taking charge of his life and of making a gift of himself as part of his commitment to celibacy. The formation of seminarians in preparation for the celibate life should be seen in the context of the vocation of all members of the Church to chastity. Chastity is defined in the *Catechism of the Catholic Church* as 'the successful integration of sexuality within the person and thus the inner unity of man in his bodily and spiritual being'.[221] This involves 'an apprenticeship in self-mastery which is a training in human freedom';[222] it is 'a long and exacting work which is never acquired once and for all';[223] it presupposes constant effort at all stages of life, but especially at certain stages, such as when the personality is being formed during adolescence.[224]

170. Every seminary has a responsibility to ensure that the human dimension of formation favours the candidate's spiritual, intellectual and pastoral formation. Priests are to be disciples, striving for holiness of life. So, 'human formation, when it is carried out in the context of an anthropology which is open to the full truth regarding man, leads to and finds its completion in spiritual formation'.[225] Priests are to be teachers and preachers of the Gospel. Therefore, 'intellectual formation has its own characteristics, but it is also deeply connected with, and indeed can be seen as a necessary expression of, both human and spiritual formation'.[226] Study and discipline are formative of the person. Study can never be just the training of the mind; it is the transformation of the human heart. It transforms the heart through discipline and learning. It offers the seminarian the rigour of remaining in his room in silence, struggling to understand, when he longs to escape. The purpose of study is not merely to gather information, but to bring the student to a moment of conversion when false images of God are destroyed so that he draws near to the mystery.

---

[219] PDV 44
[220] PDV 43 and 44
[221] CCC 2337
[222] Ibid. 2339
[223] Ibid. 2342

[224] Cf. *The Truth and Meaning of Human Sexuality: Guidelines for Education within the Family* issued by the Pontifical Council for the Family (1996)
[225] PDV 45
[226] PDV 51

171. Priests are to be pastoral ministers of the Church. In this way, 'the whole formation imparted to candidates for the priesthood aims at preparing them to enter into communion with the charity of Christ the Good Shepherd. Hence their formation in its different aspects must have a fundamentally pastoral character'.[227]

172. Human formation means fostering the capacity and willingness to grow in imitation of Jesus in love for the Father, through gradually expanding self-knowledge and awareness, especially motivation, and progressively confronting this increasing self-awareness with the person of Jesus and his mission. Thus, a candidate for the priesthood grows continuously and progressively in his personal relationship with Christ and in his commitment to the Church and to his vocation.[228] In this way a seminarian can grow from self-centred motivation towards a freedom for service in the kingdom.

173. The human formation programme must challenge the seminarian to achieve a convinced and heartfelt obedience to the truth of his own being. True freedom asks him to be master of himself and to open out to others in generous dedicated service. Since every person should take responsibility for his own actions, the seminarian in particular must be helped to foster personal responsibility in the use of money and in structuring and maintaining a daily schedule of prayer, work and leisure. Every seminarian should be encouraged to develop a spirit of collaboration with lay people, both men and women.[229] A seminarian is required to develop a capacity for choices that are clear, free and in keeping with his vocation.

174. A healthy lifestyle in the priesthood needs a balance of physical exercise, study and leisure. Given the connection between good health and physical fitness, seminarians should make sure they take regular exercise. Seminarians should also be encouraged to develop cultural interests and to take sufficient relaxation.

Norms

175. Since there is an intimate connection between human and spiritual formation, these areas while treated separately in this document, should not be viewed by formators as mutually exclusive.

---

[227] PDV 57
[228] Circular Letter *Concerning Some of the More Urgent Aspects of Spiritual Formation in Seminaries*, 100; PDV 43–50

[229] Cf. PDV 66

176. Seminaries should make available to seminarians the services of a suitably qualified vocations growth counsellor who shall have a strong Catholic faith and religious commitment. This person shall also be versed in and supportive of the Church's expectations of candidates for the priesthood, especially in regard to celibacy. The role of the vocational growth counsellor is to help seminarians integrate the four areas of formation as outlined in *Pastores dabo vobis*, namely the spiritual, the human, the intellectual and the pastoral. It is consistent with the aims of the seminary in fostering a greater maturity in the seminarians for their future priestly ministry, through being able to process what goes on for them in the day-to-day life of the seminary. The seminarians have expressed the need for such help in having skilled people available. The 'vocational growth counsellor' does not function as a spiritual director ... or as a psychologist.

177. Formation staff should have due regard for the candidate's maturity, psychological balance, strength of will and inter-personal skills and where necessary shall invite him to seek the assistance of a competent vocations growth counsellor.

178. The counselling given shall be consistent with the overall seminary programme and shall not take the place of spiritual direction.

179. There should be sufficient time for physical exercise and leisure in the schedule.

180. Effective seminary formation for celibacy presupposes appropriate psychosexual development and helps a seminarian to appreciate and develop in a wholesome manner the affective and relational dimensions of his personality.

181. In regard to all confidential material arising from psychological assessment or counselling, the seminary should observe closely all legal requirements and make use of the appropriate release forms.

Spiritual Formation

182. The seminary should provide an ethos of human and spiritual formation in which seminarians are encouraged to grow continuously and progressively in their personal relationship with Christ and in their commitment to the Church and to their vocation.[230] A well-rounded and effective programme of spiritual formation presumes and builds upon continuing theological and personal growth and character development consistent with a priestly vocation. Personal growth and character development should progress together harmoniously within a deepening spiritual life. 'For every priest, his spiritual formation is the core which unifies and gives life to his being a priest and his acting as a priest.'[231]

183. The spiritual formation programme aims to enable the student to take on the likeness of Christ. It is to be seen as a stage in a journey which has its beginning in Baptism, is life-long, under the influence of the Holy Spirit. Indeed, it 'is the work of the Holy Spirit and engages a person in his totality. It introduces him to a deep communion with Jesus Christ, the Good Shepherd, and leads to the total submission of one's life to the Spirit, in a filial attitude towards the Father and a trustful attachment to the Church'.[232] Spiritual formation of those preparing for priesthood 'should be conducted in such a way that the students may learn to live in intimate and unceasing union with God the Father through his Son Jesus Christ, in the Holy Spirit. Those who are to take on the likeness of Christ the priest by sacred ordination should form the habit of drawing close to him in every detail of their lives'.[233]

184. The goal of spiritual formation is to establish attitudes, habits and practices in the spiritual life that will continue after ordination. Spiritual formation in the seminary sets the foundation for a lifelong commitment to priestly ministry. The programme encourages a student in a way of Christian living that involves interior discipline and self-sacrifice. This leaves him free and willing to undertake obedience, celibacy and simplicity of lifestyle, understanding their value and importance in the life and ministry of the priest and seeing them as living signs

---

[230] PDV 43–50
[231] PDV 45
[232] Synod of Bishops, The Formation of Priests in the Circumstances of the Present Day, Instrumentum laboris, 20; cf. PDV 45

[233] OT 8: cf. also 9

of Christ-like love. 'The spiritual life is, indeed, an interior life, a life of intimacy with God, a life of prayer and contemplation. But this very meeting with God, and with his fatherly love for everyone, brings us face to face with the need to meet our neighbour, to give ourselves to others … following the example which Jesus has proposed to everyone as a programme of life when he washed the feet of the Apostles: "I have given you an example, that you should also do as I have done to you."'[234]

185.   During his time in the seminary the student's spiritual formation is helped and supported in various ways. The daily timetable is structured to give special emphasis to community prayer: the Eucharist, the Liturgy of the Hours, the Sacrament of Reconciliation, Rosary and other opportunities for prayer form the seminary community into a concrete instance of the Church at prayer. As such it becomes the proper setting for conversion and priestly formation. In addition, the spiritual formation programme must also help the individual seminarian to interiorise the values of the spiritual life and integrate the lessons of intellectual and pastoral formation. So it is desirable that the programme of spiritual formation form a unified and coherent whole with the other areas of the formation programme.

186.   Daily celebration of the Eucharist should be the centre of the whole life of the seminary. Seminarians should be 'trained to consider the Eucharistic celebration as the essential moment of their day, in which they will take an active part'.[235] The Rector and the seminary staff should celebrate the Liturgy together with their students, so that the community nature of the Liturgy and its richness will be made clear.

187.   A well-planned variety in the manner of celebration should be fostered and encouraged.[236] Because the liturgical life of the seminary shapes the sensitivities and attitudes of seminarians for future ministry, liturgical celebration, especially the Eucharist, should be carefully prepared and celebrated. Catechesis on the meaning and proper celebration of the Eucharist (and of the Liturgy of the Hours) is essential, and students should receive guidance in the principles of Liturgy and the norms provided in the liturgical books. In this way, a student deepens his

---

[234] PDV 49
[235] PDV 48

[236] Cf. OT 8; SC 17, 18, 19; PO 5

awareness of 'the Paschal Mystery of Jesus Christ who died and rose again and is present and active in the Church's sacraments'.[237]

188. Seminarians should be instructed in the need for daily personal prayer and 'the human meaning and religious value of silence as the spiritual atmosphere vital for perceiving God's presence'.[238] In a world of noise and ceaseless activity students need to discover the value of silence where they can truly encounter God and themselves. In this way, the seminarians maintain 'the vivacity and abundance of the moments of silence and prayer in which they cultivate and deepen their own essential relationship with the living figure of Jesus Christ'.[239] In this regard the spiritual formation programme should teach seminarians how to pray and introduce them to methods of prayer.

189. Students should be assisted in developing life-long habits of daily prayer enriched by reading and meditation on the Scriptures so that they develop an intimate relationship with Christ. 'An essential element of spiritual formation is the prayerful and meditated reading of the Word of God (lectio divina).[240] This too is essential for deepening awareness of Christ, for 'ignorance of the Scriptures is ignorance of Christ'.[241] During their years in seminary, students should be introduced to the spiritual classics and encouraged to develop a habit of fruitful spiritual reading.[242]

190. Opportunities for devotional prayer, for example, the Rosary and the Stations of the Cross, should be provided. Devotion to Mary, Mother of God, and to the saints, should be cultivated and properly explained. Instruction on the Irish saints and martyrs should be given together with an understanding of devotional practices that have grown up around their feasts and the places associated with their lives.

191. Particular attention is to be given to the meaning and practice of the Sacrament of Reconciliation as a means of conversion. Communal celebrations of the sacrament are important moments in the life of the seminary. Individual celebration of the sacrament must be available and always encouraged.[243] Seminarians who have discovered the value of the sacrament in their own lives will be more effective ministers of the sacrament as priests.

---

[237] PDV 48
[238] PDV 47
[239] DMLP 40
[240] PDV 47

[241] St Jerome, Comm. in Isaias, Prol.: PL 24, 17; cf. Benedict XV, Spiritus Paraclitus, 475–480; Pius XII Divino Afflante Spiritu: EB 544; DV 25
[242] DMLP 39
[243] CIC 960

192. The essential rhythm of the Eucharist, the Liturgy of the Hours, the Liturgical Year, sacramental reconciliation, universal and national saints' days, finds its proper continuation in other elements of the programme of spiritual formation. Direction from formation staff and spiritual directors, days of recollection, retreats and workshops on spiritual growth and human development make important contributions to the spiritual formation of seminarians.

193. The essential meaning of celibacy is grounded in Jesus' preaching of the kingdom of God. Its deepest source is love of Christ and dedication to his mission. All these elements are rooted in the unique way that Jesus spoke about God's reign and exemplified his teaching in his own life, death and resurrection. The Church is challenged in every age to articulate the theological meaning of the celibate commitment and its inner affinity to the priesthood to which the tradition of the western Church has witnessed in a special way.[244] Programmes of priestly formation and the ongoing formation of clergy are especially challenged to explain the rationale of celibacy more consciously and persuasively, and then nourish and support priestly celibate life as a sign of God's kingdom.

194. The celibate commitment remains one of the most fundamental expressions of Jesus' call to radical discipleship for the sake of the kingdom.[245] Even the highest and most cherished natural good, a family, is transformed in light of God's Kingdom. For the priest the absence of natural family together with marital and parental love, is replaced by many other ties of affection, respect and love, which take on new significance in light of God's kingdom. Priests give up one kind of family and gain another. In Christ, the people they serve become brother, sister, mother.[246] For this reason, celibacy can truly be called 'a sign and motive of pastoral charity, and a special source of spiritual fruitfulness in the world'.[247] Celibacy is not a denial of sexuality and love but a specific way of living them. Reciprocity, mutuality and affection shared with many rather than one individual or an exclusive few, become expressions of a priest's pastoral love. The celibate commitment means a consecration to God by which the priest 'adheres more easily to Christ with an undivided heart'.[248] It 'finds its ultimate motivation in the link between celibacy and sacred ordination, which configures the priest to Jesus Christ the Head and Spouse of the Church'.[249] Priestly celibacy must,

---

[244] SC 36; PDV 29

[245] LG 42

[246] Mk 3:33–35

[247] LG 42; cf. PO 16; OD 14

[248] OD 2

[249] PDV 29

therefore, 'not be considered just as a legal norm, nor as a totally external condition for admission to ordination, but rather as a value that is profoundly connected with ordination, whereby a man takes on the likeness of Jesus Christ, the Good Shepherd and Spouse of the Church, and therefore as a choice of a greater and undivided love for Christ and his Church, as a full and joyful availability in his heart for the pastoral ministry'.[250]

195.   Seminarians must understand clearly and realistically the value of celibate chastity and its connection to priestly ministry. To be lived fruitfully, the value of celibacy must be interiorised. The celibate's personal relationship with Christ through prayer and the sacraments will provide strength to meet the challenges of celibate living. The support which a seminarian receives from his brother priests and which he in turn gives to them is also an important element in celibacy lived together.

196.   As every spiritual journey is personal and individual, it requires personal guidance and discernment. Every seminarian, therefore, should have a spiritual director whose task is to assist him in his path of personal conversion to Christ in his growth in relation to the priesthood.[251] Spiritual direction represents a relationship in the internal forum which enjoys confidentiality. Seminarians should avail themselves of this unique opportunity for growth by being as honest and transparent as possible about all the areas of life with their spiritual directors and trustful and responsive to their counsel. Prayer, spiritual reading, relationship with Christ, sexuality, celibate chastity, justice, personal relationships, commitment, simplicity of lifestyle and interiorisation are among the essential topics for spiritual direction. In this setting, seminarians should be encouraged to speak about their own personal struggles and review their success and failure in living a chaste, celibate life.

197.   While it is common practice for the student's spiritual director to be his confessor, he is free to approach a confessor of his choice inside or outside the seminary.[252] In deciding about the admission of a student to orders, or his dismissal from the seminary, the opinion of the spiritual director or confessor may never be sought.[253]

---

[250] PDV 50
[251] CIC 239, § 2; cf. RF 55

[252] CIC 240 § 1; CIC 246 § 4; RF 55
[253] CIC 240 § 2

Norms

198. Spiritual formation should involve the whole person. Grace builds on nature, raising it to a higher level, and thus the human virtues become Christian ones, unified and animated by charity.

199. There shall be a daily celebration of the Eucharist in which the members of the community normally participate.

200. The seminary community shall celebrate the Liturgy of the Hours, especially Morning and Evening Prayer, on a daily basis.

201. Instruction shall be given about the meaning and proper celebration of the Eucharist and Liturgy of the Hours.

202. The preparation and execution of liturgical celebrations shall be carefully supervised.

203. Communal celebration of the Sacrament of Reconciliation shall be scheduled. Regular opportunities for individual celebration of the Sacrament must be provided.

204. Instruction shall be given concerning the importance of the Sacrament of Reconciliation and its regular celebration in the life of the priest.

205. Talks, days of recollection, retreats and workshops shall be provided and organised in order to create an overall coherent programme of spiritual formation.

206. Apart from retreats and days of recollection, an atmosphere of silence and properly directed solitude shall always permeate the seminary. Students should be encouraged and helped in developing the habits of silence and recollection.[254]

207. Devotion to the Blessed Sacrament and the Word of God should be especially encouraged in the seminary.

---

[254] OT 11

208. Devotion to the Blessed Virgin, particularly with the recitation of the Rosary, as well as devotion to the saints in the universal and national calendars should be encouraged and properly explained.

209. Every seminarian shall have a spiritual director deputed to this work by the bishop whom he visits regularly, at least once a month.

210. Seminarians should not change their spiritual director easily, but they may be permitted to do so for good and serious reasons.

211. Seminarians are encouraged to confide their personal history, personal relationships, prayer experiences and other significant topics to their spiritual director. If, for serious reason, there should be a change of director, attention shall be given to continuity in seminarians' spiritual development.

212. Careful presentation of the Church's teaching on priestly celibacy shall be given in talks, workshops, special programmes and courses.

213. Seminarians must be helped to discern if they themselves have the gift of celibacy. In their years of seminary formation, they shall give evidence of their ability to live with maturity and integrity a life permanently committed to celibacy. Before ordination they should declare their readiness to live this commitment fully.

214. Seminaries shall admit only candidates who give testimony of a sustained habit of celibate chastity prior to admission. The candidates shall also give evidence of mature psychological and psychosexual development.

215. Directors of formation and spiritual directors should share the same understanding of an integral celibate commitment and the kinds of behaviour that are counter-indicators to commitment and growth in a celibate lifestyle.

216. In preparing students to live the celibate life in both the internal and external *fora* there should be clear delineation of the kinds of behaviour that are acceptable and those that are not. Seminarians must be reminded of their responsibility towards their own good and that of the community.

Intellectual Formation

217. The purpose of the intellectual formation in the seminary is to enable the students to acquire, along with a general culture which is relevant to present-day needs, an extensive and solid learning in the sacred sciences such as can give a firm foundation to their faith, can enable it to mature and can equip them to proclaim it effectively to the modern world.[255]

218. Seminary studies may be arranged in a number of ways:

   (a)   In three distinct and successive periods of time: Arts and Sciences, where necessary; the study of Philosophy; the study of Theology.

   (b)   Arts along with Philosophy; then Theology.

   (c)   In certain circumstances, Theology studied conjointly with Philosophy.

Whichever study arrangement be adopted, the following principles should be carefully observed:

   (a)   It should always commence with an introductory course on the Mystery of Christ and Salvation History and the relation of the priesthood to them.

   (b)   If Philosophy and Theology are taught separately the relationship between them should be clearly pointed out: for example, Natural Theology and the course on the One and Triune God in Dogmatic Theology; Ethics with Moral Theology, the History of Philosophy with Church History.

   (c)   The presentation of the 'principal arguments of fundamental, dogmatic and moral theology, theology of Sacred Scriptures, of Liturgy, of Canon Law and of Ecumenism ... should not be merely

---

[255] OT 13, 17; GS 58, 62

problematic, informative and theoretical, but must lead to an authentic formation: towards prayer, communion and pastoral action'.[256]

(d)   Whether Philosophy and Theology are studied successively or conjointly, it is important that the separate status of Philosophy be respected, and that due time be allotted to it.[257]

In every arrangement of seminary studies it is necessary that some courses in literature and in contemporary scientific questions be provided.

219.   The introduction to the Mystery of Christ and to Salvation History which is to inaugurate the course of Philosophy and Theology is designed to enable the students to appreciate the purpose and scope of ecclesiastical studies, their general plan and connection with the apostolate. At the same time, it should help to give deeper roots to their own faith and give them an opportunity to understand more fully their priestly vocation.

220.   Its length and scope should be decided according to the needs and facilities of each seminary. If it should be decided to devote an entire year to an introductory or foundation course there should be incorporated into it some definite sections of the ordinary philosophical or theological course, so as to avoid the danger of too much generalisation.

221.   The professors, when teaching their own subjects, must be concerned for the internal unity and harmony of the whole corpus of doctrine which is being taught. This will prevent acquired pieces of knowledge from remaining in isolation from each other and will enable the student to see all that he has learned in relation to his future ministry. It will also create that intellectual harmony which is necessary for his own spiritual development and should give him a greater appreciation and love of theological learning.

222.   It is particularly important that students for foreign dioceses, be given some introduction to the social and cultural conditions of their future mission.

---

[256] DMLP 77   [257] CIC 250

STUDIES IN THE ARTS AND SCIENCES

223. A sound education in humanities for candidates preparing for the priesthood possesses many benefits. Such an education encourages intellectual enquiry, promotes critical thought and fosters disciplined habits of study. Education in the humanities also teaches students to communicate with others in a clear and articulate way.

224. The study of the humanities has a special value as a preparation for the study of theology. By understanding the human sciences, students can better comprehend the world in which God's Spirit acts. By grasping how faith and culture have interacted in the past, they gain some insight into the working of God's plan in larger historical events.

225. It is also beneficial to take into consideration contemporary issues of the day in intellectual, cultural, social and political life as they pertain to moral and religious topics. Such an approach stimulates students to deeper study by building on current knowledge and present interests.

226. The seminary should ensure that candidates are of sufficient academic standard to be able to follow the prescribed courses in philosophy and theology. They should normally be required to have completed second-level education and to have achieved a satisfactory standard in the Leaving Certificate Examination, GCSE or equivalent.

227. If a student entering the seminary is deficient in some essential area of his general education this deficiency should be made good during the early years of his seminary training. An example would be the proficiency in Latin which is at present required by the Church.[258]

228. Students should learn, apart from their own language, whatever modern languages are considered necessary for their current studies and their future

---

[258] Cf. OT 13; CIC 249

pastoral ministry. In particular, students for dioceses where the Irish language is used, should have the ability to instruct, preach and celebrate the sacraments in Irish.[259] In view of the developing European dimension of the Church in Ireland today, students should be encouraged to become fluent in at least one European language.

229. In addition students should be taught how to express themselves and to communicate effectively in the spoken and written word.[260] Some training in the appreciation of art and music, both sacred and profane, is also valuable as part of their general education.[261]

230. At the beginning of a student's academic formation he should be given a short course in methods of study, in the use of library facilities and of information technology.

231. Nowadays people receive their information and convictions, not only from books and teachers, but more and more through modern communication technologies. It is very important, therefore, that students should be well versed in the use of these and receive an introduction to Media Studies. In this way, they should become capable of using these methods and means to the best effect in their future apostolate.[262]

232. From their early seminary years, and increasingly as they grow older and more mature, students should be given some knowledge and experience of the social problems both of their own country and of the country in which they will work as priests.[263]

233. While allowing for the value of some pastoral work during the academic year, care should be taken that involvement in such work complements the other areas of formation.

---

[259] Cf. Pastoral Statement of the Irish Bishops on
    The Irish Language in Religious Affairs (1981)
[260] Cf. ILFS 58

[261] Cf. GS 59, 62; ILFS 57
[262] Cf. GS 61; *Christus Dominus*, 13; SC 20; ILFS 58
[263] Cf. OT 20

PHILOSOPHICAL STUDIES

234. A substantial course in philosophy is a prerequisite to the theological studies of seminarians.[264] In the words of Pope John Paul II: 'I wish to repeat clearly that the study of philosophy is fundamental and indispensable to the structure of theological studies and to formation of candidates for the priesthood. It is not by chance that the curriculum of theological studies is preceded by a time of special study of philosophy.'[265] While philosophical studies may be distributed differently over the years of seminary formation, they must be equivalent to a two-year full-time course.[266]

235. The careful study of philosophy enables students to understand the human person, the world and God in a solid and coherent way. It also helps them to appreciate scientific research and progress, and to acquire some insight into the perennial human problems of morality, life and death. It is therefore not merely a preparation for theology but contributes in its own right to the priest's human and intellectual formation.[267] As part of philosophy students should come to some understanding of humanistic disciplines like literature and psychology, which are 'linked to the sacred sciences, particularly insofar as they benefit the exercise of the pastoral ministry'.[268] What is studied in philosophy by the light of reason prepares the way for the mysteries of salvation studied in theology in the light of faith.[269] 'Only a sound philosophy can help candidates for the priesthood to develop a reflective awareness of the fundamental relationship that exists between the human spirit and truth, that truth which is revealed fully to us in Jesus Christ.'[270]

236. From the viewpoint of methodology, philosophical studies help students to develop their powers of clear critical thought and analysis. They confront them with the epistemological and ontological presuppositions of faith and knowledge. They enable them to reach a coherent vision of reality, recognising 'human reason's ability to attain truth ... as well as its metaphysical capacity to come to

---

[264] PDV 52; cf. *The Study of Philosophy in Seminaries* (1972)

[265] FR 62

[266] CIC 250

[267] CIC 251

[268] CIC 179 § 3

[269] CIC 239 § 2

[270] PDV 52; cf. Congregation for Catholic Education, *The Study of Philosophy in Seminaries* (1972)

a knowledge of God from creation'.[271] On the other hand, they help the students become critically aware of those philosophical positions that limit or deny the role of revelation. Philosophy, as an integrative discipline, helps students to grasp their entire course of studies comprehensively.

237. The study of philosophy must be thorough, systematic and based on the great Christian philosophers, above all St Thomas, in whom 'the Church's magisterium has seen and recognised the passion for truth, and precisely because it stays consistently within the horizon of universal, objective and transcendent truth, his thought scales heights unthinkable to human intelligence'.[272]

238. When this philosophical basis has been established, the students' attention should be directed towards contemporary philosophy, and especially to the schools of thought which exercise special influence in the Irish milieu, such as positivism, linguistic analysis and phenomenology, so that philosophy can be for them 'a place where Christian faith and human cultures meet, a point of understanding between believer and unbeliever'.[273]

239. The philosophical disciplines studied should include metaphysics, anthropology, natural theology, epistemology, ethics and logic, as well as the history of ancient, medieval, modern and contemporary philosophy. Since a good deal of contemporary philosophy is written as literature, the study of the Humanities should be integrated with the philosophy course. Some introduction to science and its philosophical implications should also be given. Overall, however, a sense of proportion should be observed, so that the non-philosophical subjects complement rather than compete with the core philosophical subjects. It is of particular importance that the manner of presentation of all subjects take account not only of the intrinsic importance of the matters considered, but their relevance to present-day circumstances.

---

[271] EVT 10; cf. Vatican Council I, Dogmatic Constitution, *De fide catholica, De revelatione*, can. I (DS 3026)

[272] FR 44; cf. *Aeterni patris* 109
[273] FR 79

THEOLOGICAL STUDIES

240. The study of theology is an indispensable component of the formation of candidates for the priesthood. It is clear from the opening chapter that 'the intellectual formation of candidates for the priesthood finds its specific justification in the very nature of the ordained ministry and the challenge of the "new evangelization".[274] Thus, all formation of priests is directly aimed at the work of evangelization.[275] Since a priest is ordained to serve as a teacher and shares in the mission of 'preaching the good news to the poor' in the name and person of Christ, he must proclaim and teach the 'changeless Gospel of Christ and make it credible to the legitimate demands of reason'.[276] The proclamation of the Gospel is primary in the ministry of priests who are leaders and transmitters of the faith.[277] 'The priest is first of all a minister of the Word of God. He is consecrated and sent forth to proclaim the Good News of the Kingdom to all, calling every person to the obedience of faith and leading believers to an ever-increasing knowledge of and communion in the mystery of God, as revealed and communicated to us in Jesus Christ.'[278] Consequently, a seminary is called to form candidates for the priesthood into men of the Gospel.

241. In their theological formation, students undertake the study of the revelation of God to the world, perfected in Jesus Christ and made present and actualised in and through the Church under the guidance of the Holy Spirit. Candidates for the priesthood must fully realise that 'the paschal mystery of Christ's cross and resurrection stands at the centre of the Good News that the Apostles and the Church following them, are to proclaim to the world'.[279] They search for the truth in the light of that revelation embodied in the Scriptures and in the Tradition of the Catholic Church. This mystery, however, gives access to the other central mystery of faith. The 'mystery of the Most Holy Trinity is the central mystery of Christian faith and life. It is the mystery of God. It is therefore the source of all other mysteries of faith, the light that enlightens them. It is the most fundamental and essential teaching in the "hierarchy of the truths of faith".'[280] Through a programme of theological studies candidates for the priesthood

---

[274] PDV 51
[275] Cf. PDV 2, 7, 10, 38, 59
[276] PDV 51
[277] Cf. CIC 757, 762, 776

[278] PDV 26
[279] CCC 571
[280] Ibid. 234

participate 'in the light of God's mind'.[281] Seminarians are required to follow a full theological programme in order to be able to account for their faith and hope.[282] The equivalent of at least four years must be devoted to theological studies,[283] which 'should aim to give a systematic vision of the Christian mystery, including the study of the essential themes of faith and the Christian life'.[284] The study of theology helps seminarians to develop their knowledge of all that pertains to the gospel, to penetrate more deeply its meaning and so to grow in their love for God, for the Church and for all those redeemed by Jesus Christ. Theology encourages them to ask questions about their own faith in order to reach a more profound understanding of the faith itself. In this way faith and mature reflection are intimately connected in their theological study.

242. 'The commitment to study, which takes up no small part of the time of those preparing for the priesthood, is not in fact an external and secondary dimension of their human Christian, spiritual and vocational growth.'[285] The study of theology in the seminary, therefore, is not an academic exercise separated from the other areas of formation. Theology must be 'taught in such a way that students … will nourish their own spiritual lives with it'.[286] All priests, and not just professional theologians, are called on to exercise a 'theological ministry in the Christian community'.[287]

243. The teaching of theology is always to take into account the future pastoral mission of seminarians and in particular the cultural climate in which they will minister.[288] Because they are preparing to be ministers of the Word, seminarians need an ever deeper awareness of the presence of God in our world if they are to be a witness to the faith in a society that is often marked by religious indifference, as well as by fresh questions raised by scientific and technological advances.

244. To preach effectively, seminarians must understand the world in which the message of Christ is preached. The academic programme should help them develop skills in reading the signs of the times in relation to the Gospel and the teachings of the Church. In this regard, a knowledge of history and the human sciences is invaluable. It should not be forgotten that 'theology plays a particularly important role in the search for a synthesis of knowledge as well as

[281] PDV 51
[282] Cf. 1 Pet 3:15; cf. FR 62
[283] CIC 250; TFFP 13
[284] TFFP 133
[285] PDV 51
[286] OT 16
[287] TFFP 6–8
[288] RF 91; cf. 69

in the dialogue between faith and reason. It serves all other disciplines in their search for meaning … In turn, interaction with these other disciplines and their discoveries enriches theology'.[289]

245.   Theological learning takes place within the life of faith. Through theological and scriptural studies, future priests assent to the Word of God, grow in the spiritual life and prepare themselves as pastoral ministers.[290] Consequently, a sound theological education is essentially incomplete without personal appropriation by seminarians. With such appropriation, as faith and knowledge penetrate interior understanding, intellectual conversion should follow. The study of theology and growth in the spiritual life should develop together harmoniously. Such a theological foundation blends fidelity to the Church with imagination and creativity.

246.   Every ecclesiastical faculty of theology 'has the particular mission of fostering the scientific theological training of those who are preparing themselves for priesthood'.[291] Its members should always bear in mind that their work corresponds 'to a dynamism found in the faith itself' and that the proper object of their enquiry is 'the Truth which is the living God and his plan for salvation revealed in Jesus Christ'.[292]

247.   Members of theology faculties in seminaries play an important role sharing with the formation team proper in the common task of accompaniment.[293]

248.   The teaching of theology should relate to the students' own experiences and take into account the culture in which they will serve as priests. Nowadays fewer candidates enter seminary directly from second-level education. Some come with work experience often in the caring professions, others from third-level studies. This valuable experience should be integrated into their formation. 'An overriding consideration to be borne in mind is that the whole of the intellectual formation of students must take into account their differing backgrounds. They have to be capable of understanding and expressing Christ's message in a form which has meaning for them. They are products of a certain culture and they have to translate the Christian life into terms which will be

---

[289] Pope John Paul II, Apostolic Constitution on Catholic Universities, *Ex corde ecclesiae* (15 August 1990) 19
[290] Cf. PDV 51

[291] *Sapientia christiana* 74 §1
[292] Cf. EVT 7–8
[293] Cf. PDV 66; cf. *Saprentia christiana*, 21

relevant in their own cultural ethos. Students should be helped to reflect on their own experiences in the light of the Gospel. Therefore, professors of philosophy and theology should always draw comparisons between Christian teaching and the particular ideas about God, the world and man which are enshrined in popular traditions that are held as sacred by the people concerned and, as far as possible, use these notions to enrich the wisdom of the philosophers and the understanding of the faith.'[294]

249. 'It is as if theologians must write a new chapter in theological and pastoral epistemology, beginning – methodologically – with the facts and questions of the present day, rather than the ideas and problems of the past.'[295] Therefore academic and pastoral theology should not be considered separate areas. An integrated approach should be fostered which underpins the theological formation necessary for priestly ministry in the modern world.[296]

250. However, the study of theology is not merely a response to contemporary problems: 'working in this field does not mean that theology becomes so anthropological or anthropocentric that it ceases to be the science of God and divine things. It is, on the contrary, a matter of giving greater relevance to the problems of humankind by bringing theology more up to date without, however, changing the human–God relationship.'[297]

251. The basis for addressing contemporary issues is a proper understanding of God's revelation in Christ. As such the presentation of theology must always take into consideration the reality of priestly ministry in a rapidly changing world. The student must be formed for collaborative ministry.[298] He must fully understand that as a priest he will share responsibility with the bishop and with other priests and deacons, along with all the baptised within the Catholic community and in other Christian communities, for building the kingdom of God. In this sense, the seminary itself should be a model of collaboration and communion.

252. God's revelation is the foundation of the whole formation of a priest. Therefore, both professors and students must adhere faithfully to the written and unwritten Word of God. They must love it, make it their careful study, and in it

---

[294] RF 64
[295] TFFP 60
[296] PDV 31

[297] TFFP 62
[298] Cf. LG 28

find their spiritual nourishment.[299] Tradition and Sacred Scripture form one sacred deposit of God's Word, which is committed to the Church's care.[300] Consequently, students should be given an appreciation for this Tradition as it is found in the words of the Fathers, and expounded by the other Doctors of the Church especially St Thomas Aquinas.[301] The insights of modern theologians should be constantly kept before the minds of the students.

253. Teachers of theology hold a position of service within the Church, but also one which entails great responsibility: they teach, not in their own name, but that of the Church, since it is from the Church that they have received their commission. They should keep before their eyes the special place they occupy in the Body of Christ, and always manifest a spirit of respect and submission to the Church's Magisterium. In this way they will play their part in the building up in faith of their students and the faithful.[302]

254. Teachers of theology should take into account present trends and positions of doctrine and should strive to present these in a way which is systematic, ordered and complete. They should use their rightful freedom of enquiry but they should always approach new questions with the prudence and seriousness which the weight of their office and their responsibility towards the truths of revelation demand.[303] While recognising that the church has no philosophy of her own, nor does she canonise any one particular philosophy in preference to others,[304] teachers of theology must recognise that 'the Church's Magisterium can and must authoritatively exercise a critical discernment of opinions and philosophies which contradict Christian doctrine'.[305] Moreover, in dealing with the 'principal arguments of Fundamental, Dogmatic and Moral Theology, of Sacred Scripture, of Liturgy, of Canon Law and of Ecumenism … [teachers of theology should] … bear in mind that the teaching of these matters should not be simply problematic, informative and theoretical but must lead to an authentic formation: towards prayer, communion and pastoral action'.[306]

255. In view of the fact that there exist different degrees of theological certainty, professors should make it clear in their teaching what is proven doctrine of faith

---

[299] OT 16; DV 24–26
[300] DV 10
[301] Second Vatican Council, Decree *Gravissimum educationis*, 10
[302] LG; TFFP 44–47

[303] Cf. Congregation for Doctrine of the Faith, Instruction on the Ecclesiastical Vocation of the theologian, *Donum veritatis*, (1990) 25ff
[304] FR 49
[305] FR 50
[306] DMLP 77

and what is accepted by the consensus of theologians. Basic and reliable textbooks are very desirable. In particular the *Catechism of the Catholic Church* has an important role to play in ensuring that students acquire an overall synthesis in their theological studies. In learning to distinguish theological opinion from magisterial teaching, students should learn to assess accurately the authoritative character of magisterial statements, 'which becomes clear from the nature of the comments, the insistence with which a teaching is repeated and the very way in which it is expressed'.[307] Only when doctrine which is certain has been fully expounded, should they turn their attention to an objective exposition of what is only probable or novel or their own personal theories.[308] At all times 'theologians should remember that their work corresponds "to a dynamism found in the faith itself" and that the proper object of their enquiry is "the Truth which is the living God and the plan for salvation revealed in Jesus Christ".'[309]

256.   The success of the seminary programme depends largely on the close co-operation of the academic staff, and the co-ordination of their teaching activities.[310] As far as possible the scriptural, dogmatic, moral, liturgical, historical and pastoral aspects of the various theological themes should be treated simultaneously, so that students may realise that they are learning a unified science of the faith and the Gospel. With the guidance of a Supervisor of Studies, the teachers of theology should seek to integrate and align the various courses for which they are responsible. In this way the study of theology 'should lead the candidate for the priesthood to a complete and unified vision of the truths which God has revealed in Jesus Christ and of the Church's experience of faith'.[311]

257.   This unified vision will find its expression *par excellence* in the life witness of the teaching staff and students alike who will recall that 'the theologian is first and foremost a believer and a man of faith' and that in order to form effective masters of theology they must be 'integrated with a spirituality marked by a personal experience of God. In this way a purely abstract approach to knowledge is overcome in favour of that intelligence of heart which knows how to "look beyond" and thus is in a position to communicate the mystery of God to the people'.[312]

---

[307] EVT 24; cf. LG 24 §1
[308] *Humani generis*, 19, 20, 21
[309] Cf. FR 92 and EVT 7–8
[310] OT 5, 17; SC 16

[311] PDV 54
[312] PDV 51 and cf. *The Formation of Priests in the Circumstances of the Present Day, Instrumentum laboris*, 39

258. Good academic preparation for ministerial priesthood is achieved in a balanced programme of theological formation. Such a programme should gradually introduce seminarians to more complex and specialised areas of theology.

259. Seminarians are to be instructed in the Sacred Scriptures in a manner that leads to the development of a true love of, and deep insight into, the Bible and at the same time supports and enriches their spiritual life, their study of theology, their pastoral ministry and missionary outreach, and their use of Scripture in the Liturgy, especially in preaching.[313] Since the whole of theology finds its soul in Sacred Scripture, biblical studies are fundamental to the study of theology, every branch of which draws its inspiration from the study of the *Sacra Pagina*.[314] The teaching of Scripture should be set in a theological-ecclesial context which synthesises the Church's understanding of revelation and links theology with the fundamental articles of the Christian faith.[315] It should culminate in a theology which presents 'a united vision of the Christian mystery'.[316] Furthermore, a prophetic ministry of the priest requires, above all, a knowledge and love of the Word of God without which it is shallow and ultimately empty as 'ignorance of the Scriptures is ignorance of Christ'.[317] Overall, however, balance must be preserved between the integrity of scriptural studies as a special discipline and the place of scripture as 'the soul of theology'.[318]

260. Teachers 'should communicate to their students a profound appreciation of Sacred Scripture, showing how it deserves the kind of attentive and objective study which will allow a better appreciation of its literary, historical, social and theological value. They cannot rest content simply with the conveying of a series of facts to be passively absorbed, but should give a genuine introduction to exegetical method, explaining the principal steps, so that students will be in a position to exercise their own personal judgement'.[319] Students should be helped to acquire an overview of the whole of Sacred Scripture and to develop an appreciation of the great moments in the History of Salvation. To achieve this they need an introduction to the nature of revelation and the historical character

---

[313] RF 78; ILFS 52

[314] OT 16; SC 16; LG 8; RF 78; PDV 54

[315] OT 16; DV 23; TFFP 83, 4

[316] TFFP 80

[317] St Jerome, *Comm. in Isaias*, Prol.: PL 24, 17; Cf. Benedict XV *Spiritus Paraclitus*, 475–480; Pius XII *Divino Afflante Spiritu*: EB 544; DV 25

[318] DV 24; cf. Pope Leo XIII *Prov Deus* EB 114 and Pope Benedict XV *Spiritus Paraclitus*: EB 483

[319] Pontifical Biblical Commission, *Interpreting the Bible in the Church*, III C 3

of the Bible, a firm grasp of the relationship between the Old and New Testaments, an understanding of the principal theological themes of revelation and a firm grounding in exegetical principles and methods. They should also become as familiar as possible with the texts themselves, particularly those that feature prominently in the Liturgy and which nourish priests' spirituality and preaching.

261.   There is, however, a difference between training biblical specialists and future shepherds of the Lord's flock.[320] Though the academic teaching of Scripture in universities is more technical and the formation programme in seminaries more pastoral, still the teaching of Scripture 'can never be without an intellectual dimension that is truly serious. To proceed otherwise would be to show disrespect towards the word of God'.[321]

262.   Given the limited time at a teacher's disposal it is appropriate to make use of two alternative modes of teaching: on the one hand, a synthetic exposition to introduce the student to the study of whole books of the Bible, omitting no important area of the Old or New Testament; on the other hand, in-depth analysis of certain well-chosen texts, which will provide at the same time an introduction to the practice of exegesis. In either case, care must be taken to avoid a one-sided approach that would restrict itself, on the one hand, to a spiritual commentary empty of historical-critical grounding or, on the other hand, to a historical–critical commentary lacking doctrinal or spiritual content.[322] Teaching should at the same time show forth the historical roots of the biblical writings, the way in which they constitute the personal word of the heavenly Father addressing his children with love[323] and their indispensable role in the pastoral ministry.[324] Moreover, 'students should be introduced into the correct methods of exegesis after a suitable introduction and with the support of auxiliary courses. In accordance with their needs, the professors should explain what the main problems are and their solution and really help them acquire a vision of the whole of Sacred Scripture with a clear insight into the principal chapters of the history of salvation.'[325]

[320] Pontifical Biblical Commission, *De Scriptura Sacra recte docenda*, EB 583
[321] Pontifical Biblical Commission, *Interpreting the Bible in the Church*, III C 3
[322] Cf. *Divino Afflante Spiritu*: EB 551–552; PCB, *De Sacra Scriptura recte docenda*: EB 598
[323] Cf. DV 21, 22
[324] Cf. 2 Tim 3:16; Pontifical Biblical Commission, *Interpreting the Bible in the Church*, III C 3
[325] RF. 78

263. The importance of the Fathers for theology and, in particular for understanding Sacred Scripture, is emphasised in *Dei verbum* as follows: 'There exists a close connection and communication between sacred Tradition and Sacred Scripture.'[326] Sacred Scripture which must be the soul of theology and its perpetual foundation forms an inseparable unit with sacred Tradition, 'one sacred deposit of the Word of God which is to the Church'[327] such that one cannot stand without the other. 'The words of the Holy Fathers witness to the living presence of this tradition, whose wealth is poured into the practice and life of the believing and praying Church.'[328] Therefore, 'she also rightly encourages the study of the holy Fathers of both East and West and of the sacred liturgies'.[329] 'Theology was born out of the exegetic activity of the Fathers, "*in medio Ecclesiae*", and especially in the liturgical assemblies in contact with the spiritual needs of the People of God.'[330]

264. In the 'classical' study of theology the second stage of the method is an examination of the contribution made by the Fathers of the East and West 'to the fruitful transmission and illumination of the individual truths of revelation'.[331] Their contribution is to be particularly valued because 'their work belongs to the living tradition of the Church to which, through providential provision, they have made contributions of lasting value in eras that were more favourable to the synthesis of faith and reason'.[332]

265. The Fathers are privileged witnesses of the Tradition whose writings offer cultural, spiritual and apostolic richness that makes them great teachers of the Church yesterday and today.[333] 'In the flow of living Tradition that continues from the beginning of Christianity over the centuries up to our present time, they occupy an entirely special place ... They laid down the first basic structures of the Church together with doctrinal and pastoral positions that remain valid for all times.'[334]

---

[326] DV 9

[327] DV 10

[328] DV 8

[329] DV 8, 9, 23

[330] Congregation for Catholic Education, *Instruction on the Study of the Fathers of the Church in the Formation of Priests*, 27

[331] OT, 16; cf. 1985 Synod of Bishops, *Relatio finalis* II B 2; RF 79; TFFP 89, 93

[332] RF 86

[333] Congregation for Catholic Education, *Instruction on the study of The Fathers of the Church in the Formation of Priests*, 17

[334] Ibid. 18

266. Although the sacred Liturgy does not exhaust the entire activity of the Church, it is, nevertheless, 'the summit toward which all the action of the Church is directed and at the same time the fountain from which all her power flows'.[335] 'Since the liturgy, in which "the work of our Redemption is carried on" is the outstanding means "by which the faithful express in their lives and manifest to others the mystery of Christ and the true Church", its diligent exercise and study will bestow on future priests a more solid knowledge and firmness in their faith as well as opening up for them the living experience of the Church.'[336] 'The study of Sacred Liturgy is to be ranked among the compulsory and major courses in seminaries and religious houses of studies. In theological faculties it is to rank among the principal courses.'[337] It is to be presented 'not so much in its juridical aspect as in a theological and historical context and, on the spiritual and pastoral plane, it should be linked up with the other subjects in order that the students may realise how the salvation mysteries are rendered present and operative in the liturgical ceremonies'.[338]

267. At the outset of the formation programme it is important for students to receive a suitable introduction to the Liturgy so as 'to participate fruitfully in the life of the seminary from the beginning'.[339] The Congregation for Catholic Education tells us: 'since the *"legem credendi lex statuat supplicandi"*, liturgical tradition should be so studied as to shed light upon doctrinal and disciplinary questions which are being discussed today concerning the mystery of Christ and the sacraments. Indeed, the sacred Liturgy through prayer opens up for the student the source of the Christian mystery and thus it nourishes their spiritual lives and fosters unity among the various disciplines of the theological course to a high degree.'[340] A more detailed treatment of the Liturgy is to be provided during their theological course.[341] This should deal primarily with the celebration of the sacraments, especially the Eucharist which lies at the heart of the life of the Church and where 'the Church is most fully and visibly itself'.[342] It should also treat of the Liturgy of the Hours and the Liturgical Year. The link between the Liturgy and Sacramental Theology should be evident in the way they are taught.

---

[335] SC 10
[336] *Instruction on Liturgical Formation in Seminaries*, 1
[337] SC 16
[338] RF 79
[339] Congregation for Catholic Education, *Instruction on Liturgical Formation in Seminaries* (1979), 8
[340] *Instruction on Liturgical Formation in Seminaries*, Appendix 1, d

[341] Cf. ILFS, 43–59 and appendix
[342] Catholic Bishops' Conferences of England & Wales, Ireland and Scotland, *One Bread, One Body. A teaching document on the Eucharist in the Life of the Church, and the establishment of General Norms on sacramental sharing* (1998), 19

In some seminaries it might be both convenient and desirable to have the Liturgy professor also teach the whole tract on the sacraments.[343] Indeed the Council encourages all teachers to 'expound the mystery of Christ and the history of salvation in a manner that will clearly set forth the connection between their subjects and the liturgy, and the unity which underlies all priestly training'.[344]

268. Special attention should be paid to the *Institutiones* which are found in the foreword of the Missal, the Lectionary and the book of the Liturgy of the Hours, as indeed also the *Praenotanda* which are found at the beginning of each of the revised Rites of the Sacraments.[345] In this way, students will be given 'an ever deeper grasp of the Liturgy of the Church, celebrated according to the present books and lived above all as a reality in the spiritual order'.[346]

269. Students should be brought to an understanding of the norms governing the Liturgy. They should be able to draw a clear line between what is changeable and what is, by divine institution, liturgically immutable.[347] 'Liturgical studies are to be imparted in such a way that the needs of modern times are suitably met. These are mainly theological, pastoral and ecumenical.'[348]

270. Given that the Liturgy 'is the school of the prayer of the Church'[349] it should be kept in mind that 'all genuine liturgical formation involves not only doctrine but also practice. This practice … is obtained first and mainly through the very liturgical life of the students into which they are daily more deeply initiated through liturgical actions celebrated in common.'[350]

271. Dogmatic theology is that branch of theology which organically and systematically presents a full account of Church teaching and demonstrates how each article of faith derives from Sacred Scripture and Sacred Tradition. From the outset it is essential that the theological method be firmly rooted in these sources. Thus, the treatment of dogmatic theology should begin with an exposition of its biblical sources. Where possible an inter-disciplinary approach should be adopted in co-operation with the Scripture professor.[351] There should

---

[343] Cf. ILFS 54
[344] SC 16
[345] Cf. ILFS 46
[346] VQA
[347] Cf. OT 16; SC 2, 10, 14, 15, 16; DMLP 49; cf. CIC 899, 3

[348] *Instruction on Liturgical Formation in Seminaries,* 44
[349] VQA
[350] ILFS 2
[351] Cf. PDV, 54 and OT 14

also be a careful explanation of the contribution which the 'Oriental and Latin Fathers have made to the formulation and handing down of the truths of revelation and how dogma has developed through historical progression'.[352] Dogmatic theology must also demonstrate that the Church's dogmas are compatible with reason by addressing objections from philosophy and other sciences. In this way 'theology strives to clarify the teaching of Revelation with regard to reason and gives it finally an organic and systematic form'.[353] There should also be a full, speculative study, after the mind of St Thomas Aquinas, of the mysteries of salvation and how they are related. This approach should emphasise 'the intimate bond which ties theological work to the philosophical search for truth'.[354] Students should also be taught how the mysteries of salvation are present and operative in the Liturgy.[355]

272. Dogmatic theology may also be taught by what is called the 'regressive method'. This begins with conciliar definitions and reflections and 'works backwards through the Fathers to Sacred Scripture'.[356] In this way the student can learn to read and understand Scripture in the light of the living tradition of the Church.[357] A formal treatment of the general principles of Ecumenism should be integrated into the ecclesiology module such that ecumenism is seen to be 'an organic part of the Church's life and work which must pervade all that she is and does'.[358]

273. Fundamental Theology should consider two points. Firstly, the core doctrines that underpin all Christian Life, namely the Trinity and the Incarnation. Secondly, two related but distinct topics, the sources and the warrants of the Christian faith. The sources encompass: revelation as divine communication and inspiration, Scripture and Tradition; Christ the Teacher; the role of the Apostles and their successors; and the Church as bearer and teacher of Revelation. The warrants embrace the whole range of Christian doctrines. Given its central importance, Fundamental Theology must therefore be given a well-defined place in the seminary programme.[359] In so far as fundamental theology is a necessary preparation for the gift of faith as well as the exposition of the rational foundations of faith it also overlaps with the field of apologetics.[360] The latter may be understood today as a reflection on the truths of Christianity in the face of

---

[352] RF 79
[353] EVT 21 and cf. PDV 55
[354] FR 63
[355] Cf. RF 79 and OT 16 and *Gravissimum educationis*, 10
[356] RF 79

[357] DV 8 and 9
[358] Pope John Paul II, Encyclical Letter *Ut unum sint* (1995), 20
[359] GS 62. AG 22
[360] RF 79 and GS 62

those challenges and problems of the contemporary world which indicate a 'crisis of meaning'[361] and a 'lack of confidence in truth'.[362]

274. Moral theology may be seen 'in its specific nature as a scientific reflection on the Gospel as the gift and commandment of new life, as a reflection on the life which professes the truth in love and as a reflection on the Catholic Church's life of holiness'.[363] As such moral theology must be a thorough and 'careful enquiry rooted unambiguously in the word of God'.[364] It should demonstrate the vocation of the faithful in Christ and explain their noble calling 'to bring forth fruit in charity for the life of the world'.[365]

275. Those who teach moral theology have, in this regard, a particular responsibility to set forth the Christian vision of marriage as a sign and sacrament of God's love for his people and to underscore the vital role of the family as the basic unit in the life of the Church and of society as a whole. Moral theology rightly concerns itself with the family apostolate and the principles which underpin the pastoral care of the married and those who are preparing for marriage.[366]

276. It should also endeavour to discover 'the solution to human problems in the light of revelation and make eternal truths relevant in a changing world'.[367] Such an approach presupposes a philosophical anthropology and a metaphysics of the good. 'Drawing on this organic vision, linked necessarily to Christian holiness and the supernatural virtues, moral theology will thus be able to tackle the various problems in its competence, such as peace, social justice, the family, the defence of life and the natural environment in an appropriate and effective way.'[368] While moral theology is a distinct theological discipline it should nevertheless be complemented by 'a study of spiritual theology which ... should include a study of the theology and spirituality of the priesthood and of a life consecrated to God in the following of the evangelical counsels'.[369]

---

[361] FR 81
[362] FR 5
[363] Pope John Paul II, Encyclical Letter *Veritatis splendor* (1993), 110; cf. Eph 4:15
[364] FR 98
[365] OT 16
[366] Congregation for Catholic Education, *Directives* on the Formation of Seminarians concerning Problems related to Marriage and the Family (1995)
[367] RF 79
[368] FR 98
[369] RF 79; cf. OT 19; PO 5–6; and *Christus Dominus* 15

277. Pastoral theology is concerned with the theory and practice by which the mission of the Church is carried out. It is also understood to comprise the knowledge required by the priest to carry out his ministry for the care of God's people and the celebration of the sacraments and so represents a synthesis of scriptural studies, dogmatic, fundamental, moral and spiritual theology and Canon Law. In particular, pastoral theology has to explain the theological principles of the action by which God's salvific will through the various ministries and institutions in the Church today is actually realised.[370] Pastoral theology should also embrace the study of the social and behavioural sciences as well as that of history and anthropology as it strives to develop a sense of the needs of those who are to be the object of the Church's mission of evangelisation and sanctification. This in turn will lay the foundations for a thorough grounding in the social doctrine of the Church[371] and her teachings on the pastoral ministry to the family.[372] As a general rule it should be remembered that 'the pastoral nature of theology does not mean that it should be completely stripped of its scientific nature; it means, rather, that it enables future priests to proclaim the Gospel message through the cultural modes of their age and to direct pastoral action according to an authentic theological vision'.[373]

278. Church history is a core component of the intellectual formation of the seminarian.[374] The history of the Church is studied as ancillary to the study of the Word of God as this is expounded and interpreted by the magisterium. In examining the origins and progress of the people of God, however, proper regard for the genuine scientific quality of the discipline of history must be exhibited. The history of the Church is therefore examined in such a way that the social, economic, political and cultural contexts which have influenced the course of Church history are given their due weight. Attention will necessarily focus on areas such as the development of doctrine with a view to inculcating in the student a sense of the tradition of the Church. It seems desirable that some attention will be given to the history of the Church in the area in which the students will in future minister as priests.

279. Canon Law as contained in *The Code of Canon Law* (1983) must be taught as a necessary discipline in the programme of studies.[375] It should be taught in

---

[370] RF 79; cf. OT 20
[371] OT 20; Pope John XXIII, Encyclical Letter *Mater et magistra* (1961) 4
[372] FC 1

[373] PDV 55
[374] PDV 54
[375] TCL 3, 1

relation to the Mystery of the Church, so profoundly expressed by the Second Vatican Council. In the explanation of principles and laws it should be shown that the primary purpose of the system of ecclesiastical government and discipline is the salvation of souls in accordance with the will of God.[376] The Code must be regarded as the essential instrument for the preservation of right order in individual and social life and in the Church's zeal.[377] As well as the general introduction to Canon Law, the course should include the Canon Law of individual sacraments, especially marriage.[378]

280. The missionary dimension must be present in the formation of candidates for the priesthood although they may be destined for pastoral work in regions where the church has long been established. No Christian is exempt from the universal call to mission. The Church is missionary by its very nature.[379] 'No believer in Christ, no institution of the Church can avoid this supreme duty: to proclaim Christ to all peoples ... Above all, there is a new awareness that missionary activity is a matter for all Christians, for all dioceses and parishes, Church institutions and associations.'[380] All candidates for the priesthood must be taught that 'membership in and dedication to a particular Church does not limit the activity and life of the presbyterate to that Church: a restriction of that sort is not possible, given the very nature both of that particular Church and of the priestly ministry ... for every priestly ministry shares in the universality of the mission entrusted by Christ to his apostles'.[381]

281. Ontologically, this formation to the missionary spirit is present at ordination: 'The spiritual gift which priests have received in ordination does not prepare them merely for a limited and circumscribed mission, but for the fullest, in fact the universal mission of salvation "to the ends of the earth".'[382] Thus, throughout their academic theological formation, all candidates for the priesthood must develop a missionary heart and mind and be open to the needs of the Church and of the world.[383]

---

[376] Cf. *Instruction on the Study of the Fathers of the Church in the Formation of Priests* (1989)

[377] *Apostolic Constitution on the Code of Canon Law* (1983)

[378] Cf. *On the Teaching of Canon Law to those Preparing to be Priests* (1975)

[379] AG 3 and cf. Sacred Congregation for the Evangelization of Peoples, Circular Letter to the Episcopal Conference on the Missionary aspects of priestly formation, Pentecost 1970; OT 20; PO 12; PCV 12

[380] AG 5

[381] PDV 32; cf. PO 10

[382] Acts 1: 18; PO 10

[383] Cf. LG 23, 26; S. Congregation for the Clergy, Directive Notes *Postquam apostoli* (25 March 1980), 5, 14, 23; AAS 72 (1980) 346–347, 353–354, 360–361; Tertullian, *De praescriptione*, 20, 5–9

282. Students should be encouraged to develop a 'fuller understanding of the Churches and ecclesial communities separated from the Apostolic See as a step to the re-establishment of unity'.[384]

283. 'Ecumenical co-operation in study and teaching is already desirable in programmes of the first stages of theological education, such as are given in seminaries and in first cycles of theological faculties. This cannot yet be done in the same way as is possible at the level of research and among those who have already completed their basic formation. The Catholic Church, like other Churches and ecclesial Communities, plans the programmes and courses that it considers appropriate for this purpose and selects suitably qualified directors and professors. As a rule professors of the doctrinal courses should be Catholics.[385] Thus the elementary principles of initiation into ecumenism and ecumenical theology which is a necessary part of basic theological formation are given by Catholic teachers.[386] Once these fundamental concerns of the Church about the purpose, values and requirements of initial theological training – which are understood and shared by many other Churches and ecclesial Communities – are respected, students and teachers from Catholic seminaries and theological faculties can co-operate in various ways.'[387]

284. Students may attend special courses given at institutes, including seminaries, of Christians of other Churches and ecclesial Communities, in accordance with the general criteria for the ecumenical formation of Catholic students, and subject to any norms that have been laid down by the Episcopal Conference.[388]

285. After the students have received basic formation, professors from other Churches and ecclesial Communities may be invited to give lectures on the doctrinal positions of the Churches and communities they represent, in order to complete the ecumenical formation the students are already receiving from their professors.

286. A wider field of ecumenical collaboration is open to those who are engaged in theological research and teaching on a post-graduate level than is possible on

---

[384] RF 80; Second Vatican Council, Decree on Ecumenism *Unitatis redintegratio* (1964), 9
[385] Directory for the Application of Principles and Norms on Ecumenism, 192
[386] Ibid.
[387] Ibid.
[388] Ibid. 194

the level of seminary or undergraduate teaching. The maturity of the participants and the advanced levels of study already attained bring a special security and richness to their co-operation.[389]

287.   Great care must be taken in forming students' attitudes towards the Jewish people since some biblical interpretations, theological arguments and liturgical language have contributed significantly to anti-Semitic prejudice in the past. 'The Church of Christ acknowledges that in God's plan of salvation the beginning of her faith and election is to be found in the patriarchs, Moses, and the prophets … Since Christians and Jews have such a common spiritual heritage, this sacred Council wishes to encourage and further mutual understanding and appreciation. This can be obtained, especially, by way of biblical and theological enquiry and through friendly discussions … The Jews should not be spoken of as rejected or accursed as if this followed from Holy Scripture. Consequently all must take care, lest in catechising or in preaching the Word of God, they teach anything which is not in accord with the truth of the Gospel message or the Spirit of Christ.'[390] In the teaching of Church History there should be an acknowledgement of failures in this regard in the past.

288.   'The Church also has a high regard for the Muslims.'[391] Over the centuries many quarrels and dissensions have arisen between Christians and Muslims. 'The sacred Council now pleads with all to forget the past, and urges that a sincere effort be made to achieve mutual understanding; for the benefit of all, let them together preserve and promote peace, liberty, social justice and moral values.'[392]

289.   Students should be given the opportunity to know the other world religions which may be more prominent in certain areas; to recognise what is good and true in them, and to communicate the full light of the truth to those who do not possess it.[393]

Norms

290.   Theological studies require an appropriate and sound philosophical formation. Those requirements are stated in this document in the section on Philosophy.

---

[389] Ibid. 196
[390] NA 4
[391] NA 3

[392] Ibid.
[393] RF 80; OT 16; NA 2; AG 16; EN 56

291. The academic curriculum should have a discernible and coherent unity.

292. The curriculum must reflect the specialised nature of priestly formation and assist seminarians to develop a clear understanding of the ministerial priesthood.

293. Within all parts of the curriculum, clear reference should be made to the pastoral aim of theology.[394]

294. Courses addressing the basic or foundational aspects of the theological disciplines are mandatory.

295. Each seminary should have an adequate number of qualified teachers.[395]

296. Professors should agree upon a definite number of lectures for all formal courses and on the general direction of the students' private study.

297. There should be a system of seminars and practical exercises to encourage the active participation of the students. Those whose task it is to direct these activities should ensure that they are undertaken with the same academic rigour as is required for formal lectures.

298. Students should be encouraged to develop a personal method of study.

299. Continual assessment throughout the academic year by means of essays, assignments and mid-term and final examinations, fosters a programme of constant work.

300. The provision of an adequate library of books and periodicals and ready access to modern technologies is an essential part of a sound theological programme. A comprehensive library will encourage students to practise deeper reading and reflection beyond the minimum requirements of class assignments.

---

[394] PDV 55   [395] CIC 253 § 1

301. In Scripture the core teaching material should include Introduction to Old and New Testaments, the Gospels, Epistles and Acts of the Apostles, Pentateuch, the Historical Books, Psalms and Wisdom Literature and Prophets.

302. In keeping with their ability and academic status students should be given the opportunity of learning Hebrew and Biblical Greek so that they may be able to study the original biblical texts.

303. All seminarians shall acquire a good knowledge of Latin.[396] This will enable them to read the Vulgate and consult the patristic commentaries.[397]

304. There should also be some treatment of the other supporting matters such as textual criticism and biblical history, the history of exegesis and interpretation, geography and archaeology.[398]

305. The study of the Fathers belongs to the core of theological studies and should not be treated as marginal, nor offered only as an elective subject.

306. In Dogmatic theology, the core should include Fundamental Theology,[399] Theology of God, Christology, Creation, the Fall and the Nature of Sin, Redemption, Grace and the Human Person, Ecclesiology, Sacraments, Eschatology, Mariology,[400] Missiology[401] and the Theology of Priesthood.

307. In Moral Theology, the core should include Fundamental Moral theology, Medical Ethics, Marital and Sexual Ethics, Bioethics and Social Ethics. The social teaching of the Church should be presented in its entirety with appropriate principles of reflection, criteria for judgement and norms for action. The systematic study of the social encyclicals. The virtues, and the human person as moral agent is especially recommended.[402] The sacrament of Penance should be treated from the point of view of both moral and systematic theology.

---

[396] CIC 249
[397] OT 13; RF 80
[398] RF 80
[399] Cf. TFFP 107–113
[400] Cf. *The Virgin Mary in Intellectual and Spiritual Formation* (1987)
[401] Missiology may be treated as a separate component or integrated into ecclesiology; it must form an integral part of every treatment of evangelisation
[402] Cf. *Guidelines for the Study and Teaching of the Church's Social Doctrine in the Formation of Priests* (1988)

308. Pastoral studies should be linked to other areas of theology and should avail of modern insights and developments of the relevant human sciences.

309. All students should be given a brief and suitable introduction to the Liturgy at the beginning of their time in the seminary. This introduction should treat especially of the Sacraments of the Eucharist and of Penance, the Liturgy of the Hours and the liturgical seasons. In Liturgy the core should include an Introduction to Liturgy and studies in the historical, spiritual and juridical aspects of Liturgy.[403]

310. 'Great care should be exercised in preparing the students to fulfil the office of moderator of the liturgy and president of the liturgical assembly by teaching them all things regarding a correct celebration of the liturgy, most especially Holy Mass.'[404] Special attention should be given to the Sacrament of Penance in liturgical *practica*. Seminarians should be given a solid grounding in music and its role in liturgical celebration.[405]

311. In historical studies, the core should include early, medieval, modern and contemporary Church History; and Irish Church History which should be taught in a way that reflects the origins of the Church in Ireland.

312. In Canon Law, the core should include a general introduction to Canon Law, the law that relates to the constitution of the Church and the Canon Law of individual sacraments, especially marriage.[406]

313. Students should become familiar with the universal and national directories on ecumenism, *Directory for the Appliction of Principles and Norms on Ecumenism (1993)* and the Irish Episcopal Conference *Directory on Ecumenism in Ireland (1976)* and with the other documents such as *Lumen Gentium, Unitatis Redintegratio, Nostra Aetate, One Bread One Body, Directory on Mixed Marriages* (1987).

314. During the course of their formation seminarians should become familiar in a practical way with the life and worship of other Churches and ecclesial communities. They should develop a respect for and ease of relationship with the

---

[403] Cf. Congregation for Catholic Education,
Instruction on Liturgical Formation in Seminaries
(1979)
[404] ILFS 20; cf. Sacred Congregation of Rites'
Instruction, *Eucharisticum mysterium* (1967), 20

[405] Cf. ILFS, 57
[406] Ibid.

ordained ministers and other officials in these communities, especially in those with which they will have contact in their future ministry. They should develop an understanding of the sensitivities, needs and difficulties experienced by inter-Church or inter-faith families.

315. Students should learn the basic principles of ecumenical collaboration, such as the importance and sound knowledge of, and respect for, the teaching and internal discipline of one's own Church and of the Church or ecclesial community with which one is in dialogue and collaboration for example, the different teaching and discipline regarding the Eucharist as outlined in *One Bread One Body* (1998) and its appeal for mutual respect of internal discipline or regarding mixed marriages as in *Directory on Mixed Marriages* (1987).

316. In spirituality, the core should include an introduction to spirituality, a selection of classic spiritual writers and an introduction to spiritual direction.

317. Homiletics should occupy a prominent place in the core curriculum and be integrated into the entire course of studies. In addition to the principles of biblical interpretation, catechesis and communications theory, seminarians need to learn those practical skills needed to communicate the Gospel in an effective and appropriate manner.

318. Throughout the academic curriculum, questions of theological methodology should be emphasised so that students learn to evaluate the strengths and limitations of various theological viewpoints.

319. All methodologies employed should be clear on the distinction and relation between truths revealed by God and contained in the deposit of faith, and their theological mode of expression.[407]

320. The normative function of the magisterium should be presented as a vital, integral and essential component of the theological enterprise.

---

[407] Cf. The International Theological Commission,
    On the Interpretation of Dogma (1989)

321. Theological formation in seminaries should clearly respect traditional doctrinal formulations of the faith while exploring contemporary modes of theological expression and explanation. Undue attachments to older theological currents or hasty assimilation of new ones should be avoided.

322. Theological education for the priesthood should resist any tendency to reduce theology to a merely historical or sociological investigation or a study of comparative religions.

323. The entire academic programme should make seminarians aware that they have a responsibility to continue their theological and pastoral education after ordination.

324. Degrees and diplomas should be available to students who satisfactorily complete a specified course of studies in the seminary. To this end, it is recommended that seminaries in this country should, with the approval of the competent ecclesiastical authority, seek affiliation with the Pontifical University of Maynooth or other recognised authorities for the granting of degrees or diplomas.[408]

325. Before proceeding to the next year of his programme a seminarian, in addition to having attended the prescribed courses, must attain the requisite standard in examinations.

326. Diocesan bishops and religious superiors should be encouraged to designate students who complete their basic programme with honours for further study.

327. Academic ability is not the sole criterion for post-graduate studies: suitable qualities of character are also essential.[409]

328. Contemporary techniques and use of the modern education technologies should be encouraged.

---

[408] Cf. *Normae quaedam* 47; *Gravissimum educationis* 12; GS 62   [409] OT 18

Pastoral Formation

329. The whole formation imparted to students for the priesthood aims at preparing them to enter into communion with the charity of Christ, the Good Shepherd. Thus, the entire programme in a seminary must have a 'fundamentally pastoral character'.[410] It is geared to enabling the priest to be a genuine shepherd of the flock modelling himself on the life and ministry of Christ, the Good Shepherd. 'Pastoral theology is not just an art. Nor is it a set of exhortations, experiences and methods. It is theological in its own right, because it receives from the faith the principles and criteria for the pastoral action of the Church in history.'[411] In other words, pastoral formation must be rooted in pastoral theology.

330. Throughout their time in the seminary, students are gradually introduced to a co-ordinated pastoral programme that provides practical experience, reflection and participative learning. 'Pastoral formation certainly cannot be reduced to a mere apprenticeship, aiming to make the candidate familiar with some pastoral techniques. The seminary which educates must seek really and truly to initiate the candidate into the sensitivity of being a shepherd, in the conscious and mature assumption of his responsibilities, in the interior habit of evaluating problems and establishing priorities and looking for solutions on the basis of honest motivations of faith and according to the theological demands inherent in pastoral work.'[412]

331. The Second Vatican Council's *Decree on the Training of Priests* insists on the co-ordination of the different aspects of formation – human, spiritual and intellectual.[413] 'At the same time it stresses that they are all directed to a specific pastoral end. This pastoral aim ensures that the human, spiritual and intellectual formation has certain precise content and characteristics; it also unifies and gives specificity to the whole formation of future priests.'[414] The pastoral aspect of seminary formation, therefore, is seen as having a co-ordinating and unifying role with regard to the other aspects of formation.

---

[410] Cf. OT 19; PDV 57–59
[411] PDV 57
[412] PDV 58

[413] OT 4
[414] PDV 57

332. So for pastoral formation to be complete, it must be organised 'not as something haphazard, but as a systematic offering of subjects, which unfolds by stages and takes on precise forms'.[415] In order for this 'to be truly fruitful and to attain its formational objective needs to be oriented and co-ordinated by a well-experienced priest assigned expressly to this ministry. He should familiarise himself with certain principles of effective supervision and evaluation of such activities and be inspired by the genuine principles of the sacred ministry in conformity with the norms of ecclesiastical authority. The priest with this duty, called director or co-ordinator of pastoral activities, should be respectful of the disciplinary arrangement of the seminary, proceeding in strict collaboration with the rector, with the other educators and teachers and, in particular, with the professor of pastoral theology'.[416]

333. The difference between pastoral experience and pastoral reflection needs to be borne in mind. Of itself pastoral experience is not sufficient unless the seminarian is able to reflect on it and learn from it. Therefore, the principal objective of the pastoral formation programme is to enable seminarians to reflect upon their pastoral experience to see how theology and the tradition of the Church throw light on modern pastoral situations and to help them gain vital practical skills. To this end, every student should reflect regularly on his pastoral experience. Such reflection by the individual seminarian is crucial, since the candidate himself is a necessary and irreplaceable agent in his own formation. Pastoral formation should 'be studied therefore as the true and genuine theological discipline that it is: *pastoral or practical theology*'.[417]

334. Students must also be helped to see the spiritual aspect of their pastoral engagement so that they successfully continue their ministry with prayerful reflection. In this way prayer and pastoral experience are integrated with personal life and theological reflection. Intellectual, human, spiritual and pastoral formation thereby reinforce one another. This mutual interaction also helps seminarians to sense the presence of God in their pastoral engagements and to relate their life in Christ to the service of God's people. Such learning can represent a significant moment of personal integration for seminarians so that they are helped to come to terms with their own faith.

---

[415] PDV 79
[416] DPSE 63

[417] PDV 57

335. Since pastoral formation unifies the human, spiritual and intellectual formation, it forms an integral part of the overall education of the seminarian. Firstly, it challenges seminarians to give an active expression to their faith and love, and in turn, to recognise how God's love works in the lives of his people. When seminarians share, articulate and reflect on these experiences, they discover a depth to their developing spiritual life and are provided with a wealth of content for their prayer. Secondly, it offers seminarians an ongoing realistic look at the foundation of their expressed desire to move into priestly life and a base upon which to make decisions prudently and intelligently.

336. Pastoral formation provides an opportunity for seminarians to exercise leadership in the Church and to appreciate the priestly dimension of pastoral ministry. Good role models are the best teachers, as they show how active pastoral ministry can be combined with a life of prayer and Gospel simplicity. Working with priests and others who reflect the spirit of Christ reinforces a priestly vocation. Learning by example and identification is an aspect of education often used in other walks of life and is of great importance in the pastoral formation of seminarians. Co-operation and mutual understanding on the part of secular and religious priests is essential for effective ministry.

337. Pastoral formation also provides an opportunity for collaboration. 'It is particularly important to prepare future priests for co-operation with the laity.'[418] The future priest has to appreciate the specific vocation and mission of the baptised People of God. 'Seminarians are to prepare themselves carefully in order to be able to promote the vocation and mission of lay people.'[419] With a spirit of faith the future priest 'must recognise and diligently promote the various charisms of the laity'.[420] The Second Vatican Council invites priests to learn to 'recognise and promote the dignity and responsibility of the lay members of the Church, to assign duties to them in the service of the Church and to encourage them to undertake tasks on their own initiative'.[421] Future priests need to prepare for being 'inserted into the living pastoral tradition of a particular Church'.[422] Thus, students should be given, as far as possible, an understanding of the pastoral situation and needs of the diocese in which they will later work as priests. It is therefore desirable that the student should be given a variety of

---

[418] PDV 59
[419] Synod of Bishops (1977), 40; cf. CL 61
[420] Cf. Pope John Paul II, *Letter to Priests* (1989)

[421] LG 37 and cf. CL 22
[422] PDV 59

pastoral assignments under competent supervision. Supervisors should be made aware of their role in the students' formation for the priesthood and review their progress on a regular basis with the seminary pastoral director.

338. Of course it is not realistic or desirable for every seminarian to obtain experience in all pastoral fields and a good pastoral programme will promote learning through reflection or experience and not a mere multiplication of experiences. It is nonetheless important that pastoral programmes in the seminary offer the student some experience in the more essential areas viz. parochial administration, youth work, pastoral care of the family, the sick, the elderly, the imprisoned, the travelling community and migrants. It is also desirable that seminarians have some introduction to ecumenical ministry. In each of these areas, pastoral engagement is a necessary and indispensable complement to the study of pastoral theory, for such engagement helps seminarians gain pastoral skills. Such skills as are necessary for evangelisation, catechesis, counselling and group facilitation may depend in some measure on natural ability but they can also be taught. The communication of such practical skills is an indispensable aspect of seminary formation.

339. 'Seminarians need to learn the art of exercising the apostolate not only in theory but also in practice. They have to be able to pursue their assignments both on their own initiative and in concert with others.'[423] They should therefore seek to bring their theological formation to bear in a wholesome and fitting manner upon the various pastoral duties which they undertake. In particular they should draw on the insights of pastoral theology, catechetics, homiletics, liturgical and sacramental practice and Canon Law. In this way they learn to develop a pastoral skill and sensitivity and a capacity to 'identify with the joys and hopes, the grief and the anxieties of the people of this age'.[424] This is of the very essence of the cura animarum – that central aspect of the priestly calling which enjoins the priest to provide for the spiritual well-being of the people of God.

340. Where pastoral formation is a 'learning through experience' programme, seminarians must appreciate the need for a definite limitation on involvement in particular pastoral assignments and also to disengage themselves from one form of pastoral activity so that they might move to another.

---

[423] OT 21   [424] GS 1

341. It is important to prepare seminarians to be proficient in the vast array of modern media technologies and techniques; this includes the ability to make known their views in the audio, visual and print media, and an ability to avail of the vast resources offered by information technology. As well as coming to an understanding of how modern media functions, seminarians must also cultivate an awareness of the influence of the media and 'its effects upon society and culture'.[425] However, proficiency in modern technologies can never be a substitute for effective preaching. Proclaiming the Word of God is a 'primary task of all ordained priests, not only within the Church but also to the world'.[426] Here too the pastoral formation should strive to integrate the seminarian's pastoral activity with his intellectual formation so that his preaching is the fruit of a rich synthesis of all his theological and pastoral reflection.

342. Instruction should be given in the psychology of youth and adolescence, parenthood, illness, death and bereavement. Every seminarian should acquire the art of listening and the skills of counselling and know the limits of his competence and the occasions when referral to professional counsellors is required. Professional persons should be involved in this part of the formation programme.[427]

343. Pastoral experience will be of little avail to the student unless it is accompanied by continual reflection, analysis, discussion and prayer. Analysis and reflection may usefully take place in a group format with peers and with facilitation by suitably trained personnel. Such a format can help the student to reflect constructively on his pastoral placement, encouraging him to integrate his theological education with his pastoral practice and to become aware of the ways in which his ministry affects others. Indeed, students must be helped to see the theological and spiritual aspects of pastoral situations and problems, so that they may become well-balanced priests, successfully combining prayer and ministry.[428]

344. The location of the seminary will largely determine what constitutes a practical pastoral programme. As far as possible students should be given opportunities to undertake a variety of pastoral work. The programme of pastoral

---

[425] *Communio et progressio*, 111
[426] PO 4

[427] OT 20; AA 25; *Christus Dominus*, 17; LG 33
[428] Cf. PDV 58

placements may operate concurrently with the regular academic and seminary formation programme, or it may be organised around intensified periods of supervised ministry.

345. The well-structured concurrent programme of pastoral placements allows students to experience a wide variety of pastoral situations while participating in regular theological reflection in the seminary. Such a programme should allow for a progression both in terms of the difficulty of the placement and the depth of the subsequent analysis of the pastoral experience itself. It also allows the students to see the importance of their theological studies as reflected in the experience of their placements.

346. A more intense period of supervised ministry as part of the formation programme may take the form of an extended pastoral placement. Such a placement, normally for a full year after the student has begun his study of theology, can offer the student many valuable opportunities. He can develop particular personal qualities and pastoral capacities and test his own fitness for the priestly life and ministry.[429] However, a clear idea of the aims, nature and motives of such a placement needs to be discussed and developed between the formation personnel, the individual student and those responsible for his supervision while on placement.

347. An extended pastoral placement offers seminary personnel the opportunity to observe the seminarian in a ministerial situation over time. It provides occasion for guidance and formation at an important learning moment. The evaluation by the student's supervisor in the placement as well as the observations of those who served alongside him and who were served by him, should be sought.

348. Many dioceses place students in a parish or other pastoral placement for a period during the summer holidays. Such a placement offers the student an opportunity of experiencing ministry in the diocese in which he hopes to serve. It affords him contact with diocesan personnel and allows them to get to know him. To realise the full benefit of summer placements in the programme of

---

[429] Cf. OT 12; RF 42

pastoral formation, the seminary's director of pastoral formation should collaborate with the appropriate diocesan personnel. Guidelines, resource material, evaluations and general direction may be provided by the seminary to help monitor such experiences. At the end of the placement it is important that balanced and honest diocesan evaluations from supervisors and others in the pastoral placement are prepared for the appropriate seminary personnel.

349. After ordination to diaconate, it is desirable that candidates for priesthood, under the guidance of a pastor, should begin the practice of the ordained ministry.[430] Placements for deacons should follow the prescriptions of the *Code of Canon Law* and should be co-ordinated by the director of pastoral formation in the seminary.

350. Seminaries or dioceses may encourage or require participation by students in a supervised and accredited clinical pastoral experience, usually in a hospital setting. Such programmes can prove beneficial to the student, helping him to integrate the various aspects of his formation through a combination of experience of ministry and reflection on the experience. It is important for the Catholic sacramental dimension of pastoral care to be integral to the programmes in which seminarians participate.

Norms

351. The entire seminary programme should have a pastoral emphasis.

352. There should be a progressive programme of pastoral activity covering the seminarians' course which is 'always in harmony with their educational commitments'.[431]

353. Pastoral placements should be chosen with the following in mind: (a) they are near the seminary; (b) they give an opportunity for significant ministerial endeavour; (c) the commitment can be easily integrated into each student's schedule for the year; (d) there is a reliable person in charge in the placement who acts as a guide and mentor.

---

[430] Cf. OT 12
[431] PDV 57

354. All persons involved in the various aspects of the programme should liase with the director of the programme. The director should be competent in theology, have pastoral experience and be skilled in facilitating theological reflection on the goals, methods and difficulties of pastoral experience. Good supervision is essential to ensure that pastoral experience remains systematically educative and formative. The director of the pastoral programme may invite other members of the academic and formation staff, according to their fields of competence and personal skills and interests, to become involved in the pastoral programme.

355. Supervision, reflection on experience and evaluation are necessary components of an effective pastoral programme. Pastoral formation should heighten a student's interest in a life of ministerial service to the people of God.

356 Supervisors of students in placements should be chosen with care. They should have a clear understanding of the expectations of the seminary and the seminarian with regard to the placement.

357. In addition to supervisors, others collaborating in the various ministries, as well as those served, may be asked to participate in the evaluation of seminarians in their placements.

Chapter IV

Ongoing Formation

358. The divine call to perfection[432] and the task of becoming like Christ the High Priest will always be before us. Formation does not end at ordination, instead the environment in which it is undertaken changes. As is the case in the seminary, so too in the life of the priest, ongoing formation cannot be limited to intellectual formation. In other words, all four areas of priestly formation have to be taken into account with particular emphasis on the nucleus of priestly ministry – the spiritual life. In this way one can say that 'the spiritual life of the priest and his pastoral ministry go hand in hand with the ongoing personal formation to deepen and harmonise the human, spiritual intellectual and pastoral aspects of his formation'.[433]

359. Continuing formation therefore presents itself as a vital aspect of priestly life which enables the priest to achieve the twofold aim of his vocation: the service of God and of his people. It is the priest's personal response to the invitation 'to rekindle the gift of God that is within'.[434] It is also a reminder to him of the dynamism of divine grace which has been poured out and continues to be poured out in his life as a priest. The priest 'is marked permanently and indelibly in his inner being as a minister of Jesus and of the Church ... and ... comes to share in a permanent and irreversible way of life'.[435]

360. The very nature of the sacrament of Orders is such that it confers not only a share in Jesus's saving power and ministry but also in his pastoral love. Moreover, this conferring of grace is continuously renewed as God gradually reveals his saving plan in the historical development of the priest's life and it is the priest's task in turn to continue to discern God's will for him. In this way we

---

[432] Cf. Mt 4:48   [434] 2 Tim 1:6
[433] DMLP 70   [435] PDV 70

can see 'that the proper foundation and original motivation for continuing formation is contained in the dynamism of the Sacrament of Holy Orders'.[436]

361. Continuing formation is the natural corollary of a continuing vocation and a continual conversion to the *sequela Christi*. The particular following of Christ, which is priestly life and ministry, is proclaimed in a striking way in the Rite of Ordination but it must also find real expression in the priest's life and mission and his willingness to grow and develop. Ultimately 'the activity of formation is based on a dynamic sign intrinsic to the ministerial charism which is permanent and irreversible in itself. Therefore, this can never be considered finished'.[437] The sacrament of Orders is a dynamic sign which finds expression in the priest's life and mission. As the life of Christ was consecrated to the authentic proclamation of the loving will of the Father, so too the life of priests should be consecrated in his name to that same proclamation 'in word and in deed'.[438]

362. Since the task of 'transmitting the faith means awakening, proclaiming and deepening the christian vocation',[439] it is all the more important that the priest is himself seriously committed to deepening his own vocation. In a very real way this type of commitment is a demand of justice and of pastoral charity. In justice the priest owes it to the people of God to exercise the *munus pastorale* in an effective and professional manner. For this reason the Church speaks of continuing formation as a 'right duty of the priest which is established in universal law'.[440] In charity the priest is called to an 'even deeper knowledge of the mystery of Christ which is unfathomable in its richness ... and ... an even deeper knowledge of the hopes, the needs, the problems and the sensibilities of the people to whom he ministers'.[441]

363. In dedicating and committing himself to a process of continuing formation, the priest constantly renews himself in his service of 'leading in love and in strength'.[442]

364. Ensuring his continuing formation is primarily the responsibility of the priest himself.[443] If it is to be ongoing, systematic and complete he will need assistance and encouragement in realising this responsibility. In the first place, it

---

[436] PDV 70
[437] DMLP 73
[438] Cf. Jn 17:4; Heb 10:7–10; Acts 1:1
[439] PCTM 2.2

[440] DMLP 72; cf. CIC 279
[441] PDV 70
[442] PTCM 4, 3
[443] Cf. PDV 79

is desirable that each diocese (or the dioceses of a region, depending on the number of priests and the resources available) develops a programme of continuing formation taking the age and needs of priests into account and keeping an eye to current pastoral issues and changing cultural circumstances in which the Gospel is preached.[444] The establishment of such a programme ensures 'that ongoing formation is not something haphazard but a systematic offering of subjects, which unfold by stages and take on precise forms'.[445]

365. The role and responsibility of the bishop in the continuing formation of the priests under his care is of the utmost importance. This responsibility is constituted from the special relationship that exists between the bishop and his priests due to 'the fact that priests receive their priesthood from him and share his pastoral solicitude for the People of God'.[446] So the bishop should enunciate clear policies on continuing formation so that priests will be aware of the expectations of the diocese as well as of the programmes and resources available. Not alone should he establish a programme, but by word and example, the bishop should encourage priests to take seriously their own continuing formation. 'The bishop will live up to his responsibility, not only by seeing to it that his presbyerate has places and times for ongoing formation, but also by being present in person and taking part in an interested and friendly way.'[447] Indeed, 'experience teaches that the more the bishop is committed to his own formation and convinced of its primary importance, the more he will know how to encourage and sustain that of his clergy'.[448] The planning, provision, supervision and frequent revision of a suitable programme of continuing formation might fruitfully be entrusted by the bishop to a director or a group of directors. It would be the task of such a group 'to help the bishop to set the topics to be considered each year in any of the areas of ongoing formation; to prepare the necessary aids; design the courses, sessions, meetings and retreats; and organise the calendar properly so as to foresee the absences and replacements for priests'.[449]

366. The task of continuing formation, by its nature, asks the co-operation of the entire presbyterate. Aspects of the task will involve many or all the priests of the diocese – for example, retreats and days of recollection.[450] At other times priests

---

[444] Cf. PDV 79; DMLP 77
[445] PDV 79
[446] PDV 79; cf. DMLP 89
[447] PDV 79; cf. DMLP 89

[448] DMLP 89
[449] DMLP 90
[450] Cf. PDV 80

may be working together in small groups – for example, in reflecting on their pastoral experience or in the study of theology.[451] Priests should encourage each other in fraternal solicitude to continue the human, spiritual, intellectual and pastoral areas of their formation so that together and united with the bishop, they provide worthy service to the entire People of God. In this regard, should the particular formation needs of a priest require his temporary absence from his place of ministry, the understanding, co-operation and commitment to continuing formation of the presbyterate should help him realise his responsibility.

367. Particular formation needs arise for priests at different ages. Continuing formation is important for priests in the first year of their ministry. Nowadays the transition from seminary to ministry requires a suitable support structure, with appropriate guides and teachers.[452] In this regard, the Ordinary should take particular care in deciding a new priest's first appointment. 'Through frequent and regular meetings – of sufficient duration and held within a community setting, if possible – [young priests] will be assured of having times for rest, prayer, reflection and fraternal exchange. It will then be easier for them, right from the beginning, to give a balanced approach, based on the Gospel, to their priestly life.'[453]

368. Continuing formation is desirable also for priests of middle age. 'They can face a number of risks, precisely because of their age, as for example, an exaggerated activism or a certain routine approach to the exercise of their ministry.'[454] Continuing formation at this stage can provide the priest with an opportunity to reflect on his ministry thus far and renew his motivation and sense of purpose in the service of Christ and his Church.[455] This may be particularly important at an age when the priest assumes full responsibility for a parish. 'It is ... important that these priests benefit from special and thorough sessions of formation in which, apart from pastoral and theological subjects, all other psychological and emotional difficulties that may arise in that period are examined.'[456]

369. Some continuing formation is also important for priests later in life, particularly as they approach retirement. 'Ongoing formation for these priests

---

[451] Cf. PDV 80
[452] DMLP 93
[453] PDV 76

[454] PDV 77
[455] Cf. DMLP 94
[456] DMLP 94

will not be a matter so much of study, updating and educational renewal, but rather a calm and reassuring confirmation of the part which they are still called upon to play in the presbyterate not only inasmuch as they continue, perhaps in different ways, their pastoral ministry, but also because of the possibilities they themselves have, thanks to their experience of life and apostolate, of becoming effective teachers and trainers of other priests.'[457]

370.   For all priests, whatever their age or length of service it is important to keep in mind that 'ongoing formation presents itself as a necessary means to the priest of today in order to achieve the aim of his vocation: the service of God and his people.'[458]

---

[457] PDV 77   [458] DMLP 71